Freud and Human Nature

VALUES AND PHILOSOPHICAL INQUIRY

General Editor: D. Z. Phillips

Also in this series

Freud and
Human Nature

İlham Dilman

Basil Blackwell

First published 1983
Basil Blackwell Publisher Limited
108 Cowley Road, Oxford OX4 1JF, England

British Library Cataloguing in Publication Data

Dilman, İlham
    Freud and human nature.—(Values and philosophical
    inquiry)
    1. Freud, Sigmund   2. Sexual behaviour
    I.   Title   II. Series
    155.3   BF692

    ISBN 0-631-13373-9

Typesetting by Styleset Limited

Printed in Great Britain by
The Pitman Press Ltd, Bath

Contents

Acknowledgements

I am grateful to Professor D. Z. Phillips for his many helpful comments and those of two philosophers, anonymous to me, who read my manuscript for Basil Blackwell Publisher.

I would also like to thank Mrs Eileen Wimmers for typing the manuscript.

Introduction

Freud thought of the person or 'self' as made up of an ego, id and super-ego — an idea which I discuss in another book, *Freud's Conception of the Mind*. He thought of the ego as having to mediate between the demands made on it by the id and the super-ego as well as by the environment. The id represents that aspect of man in which he is at one with nature. This, he thought, is constituted by his instincts. Among these sexuality has a prominent position as a force for life. The super-ego represents the moral precepts which he has assimilated and 'internalized' from the culture of his society. Here, in a nutshell, we have the subject-matter of the present book: Freud's conceptions of sexuality and morality, their relations to a human nature which Freud conceived of as having an existence independent of what comes to man from the society in which he develops as an individual, and his conception of this development.

On all these questions I develop a way of reading Freud which is different from and opposed to what may be characterized as the popular reading of him. The latter is guided by the surface structure of his thinking, shaped by philosophical presuppositions and prejudices which need criticism. My view is not so much that this reading is wrong as that it is either superficial or one-sided and fails to reach the substance of what Freud had to say about man or the good in it, the wheat as opposed to the chaff.

I criticize Freud's hedonistic conception of sexuality and his quasi-mechanistic view of its 'components' and their 'organization', the way he represented the relation between love and sexuality, and between sexuality and the whole person, the kind of universality he attributed to the Oedipus complex, his negative conception of morality as a repressive force, his identification of conscience with the super-ego, the way he opposed human nature and culture, and the terms in which he thought about them, his biological conception of human development through the stages of the transformations of the libido, and his exclusive emphasis on the defensive role of character. The popular, and perhaps orthodox, view is that when all this has been criticized Freud is left with no leg on which to stand. My view in the book is that, on the contrary, a critique of all this will clear the way to an appreciation of Freud's real contribution.

Let me expand this a little and highlight the main features of the reading with which I replace the popular view of Freud by way of guiding the reader through the discussion of the book. Freud thought of sexuality as one of the polarities of human life, at once pleasure-seeking and binding human beings together — 'object-seeking' as Fairbairn puts it. But he did not recognize the incompatibility of these two characterizations. It is the latter characterization that he has in mind when he says that by sexuality he understands that force in human life which seeks 'to preserve and unite', and that he uses the term 'exactly in the sense in which Plato uses the word "Eros" in his *Symposium*' (Freud, 1950, vol. v, p. 280).

Most readers of Freud would say that this is not true. Simone Weil, for instance, points out that in Plato carnal love is a degraded form of chaste love, whereas in Freud chaste love is a sublimated form of carnal love (Weil, 1953, p. 69). Guntrip, an associate of Fairbairn, makes a similar point: 'Freud has to resort to the theory of aim-inhibited instincts and sublimation to conjure altruistic impulses out of non-altruistic human nature' (Guntrip, 1977, p. 79). His point is that Freud would not have needed to do so had he recognized that sex can be an expression of love and did not think of love as merely an expression of sex. This is a justified criticism, as I try to show in my discussion of Freud's conception of sexuality and his conception of love (chapters 1 and 3).

While it is incontrovertible that there is an intimate connection between sex and pleasure, Freud's emphasis on it is to be faulted for the way he connects them and confines sex to pleasure. He tends to represent it as mere sensuality, not recognizing how much sexuality is an emotion — which makes a radical difference to our conception of it and so to the possibilities inherent to it. Unless one thinks of sexuality under the aspect of love one cannot make a case for representing it as 'a force for life', one which heals and unites. Yet Freud does want to make such a case, for he did think of sex as a force of unity among human beings which he later opposed to a force for death or aggression. I am thinking of the side of his thought which has been developed in what may be called 'the object-relation tradition in psycho-analysis'.

My claim is that it is possible to read what Freud says on sex differently, even though admittedly the conceptual framework of his *Three Essays on the Theory of Sexuality* makes this difficult. It is possible to find in what he says a different trend of thought which, taken together with other things he has said, is more consonant with the spirit of psycho-analysis. It is this: a purely hedonistic sexuality, one that is confined to pleasure-seeking, is an infantile form of sexuality, though even infantile sexuality has more to it than this (see Winnicott 1958). It may persist in adult life and colour the sexuality to be found there, but this is a symptom of arrested development, an expression of something which the adult has failed to outgrow. Alternatively, it may be a defensive return to an earlier mode of sexuality, a 'regression' in the face of certain difficulties in relationship. Freud thought of the adult individual as formed through a process of development which involves the relinquishment of narcissism, hedonism, egotism and dependence. Hence, despite appearances to the contrary, he did not think of hedonism as an inevitable feature of human life, but as one which is to be lived through and overcome. The idea of it as 'inevitable' has a purely philosophical origin in Freud's thought and comes from philosophical confusion. So I describe it as 'philosophical froth'. It is not an essential part of what he had to say.

I speak of this reading as being 'more consonant with the spirit of psycho-analysis'. While there is no doubt that what I have described is part of Freud's thinking, what one discerns as the spirit of psycho-analysis is a matter of the overall view one takes of psycho-analysis, of what one makes of it. This is a matter of responsible judgement. When I speak of a particular reading of Freud's claims on a particular matter as being consonant with the spirit of psycho-analysis and then admit that what spirit one discerns there is itself responsible to one's reading there is no vicious circle involved in my argument. I spoke of *responsible* judgement. The point is that it is open to substantiation in terms of what is to be found in the corpus of Freud's thinking — in what he wrote and in his practice.

Freud speaks of sex as made up of components and he depicts its fragmentation in adult life in the form of 'perversions', as well as the 'fusion' of these components and their 'organisations' under the aegis of 'genital sexuality'. But the quasi-mechanical form in which he represents these matters prevents Freud from making sense of the connection between the wholeness of sex and the significance it can have in human life. Therefore, while this mode of representation needs criticism, this fact should not prevent us from appreciating that what is represented quasi-mechanically in his theoretical writings is the same as what he describes in his therapeutic work as the integration of the self. Freud knows well that it is in the transformation of what is thus integrated that a person finds new possibilities of sense. This is, after all, one of the cornerstones of psycho-analytic therapy.

With regard to infantile sexuality I try to show that while Freud's arguments for it were weak and, therefore, open to criticism, this does not invalidate their conclusion. I consider here, as I also do in chapter 2, Malinowski's criticisms of Freud in *Sex and Repression in Savage Society*. This book contains a careful presentation of ethnographical material against which Freud's claims about infantile sexuality and the Oedipus complex are tested. It is, in fact, a searching examination of Freud's conception of infantile sexuality and the universality of the Oedipus complex. It also contains penetrating philosophical reflections on the relation between 'instinct' and 'culture' that are critical of Freud. Nevertheless, Malinowski shows deep sympathy for the importance which Freud attached to the child's early relationships in the context of the family for his or her development. This is my reason for giving prominence to Malinowski's book, particularly in chapter 2 where I consider the role which Freud accorded to the Oedipus complex in his accounts of human development as well as the growth of civilization — the former of which is the centre of my interest in that chapter.

In chapters 4 to 6 I discuss questions relating to Freud's estimate of morality, his conception of it as a force of repression, his account of the development of the super-ego and its relation to conscience, his idea of human nature and culture as essentially opposed and irreconcilable, and the particular view he took of the character of man's nature — his hedonistic conception of it, the place he accorded to aggression in human life, and the way he linked it with morality conceived of as a repressive force.

The philosophical confusions behind Freud's estimate of morality are familiar ones. My first concern is simply to expose them and to point out that they do not take over Freud's thought entirely. He remains ambivalent in his estimate of morality and its place in human life. I then consider the kind of connection and near identity Freud sees between the super-ego and conscience, and I distinguish between two different views that can be discerned in his thinking about the way in which the super-ego is formed. The cruder view lies on the surface, and the subtler and more interesting one can be discerned beneath it, and needs developing. On the former view moral learning consists mainly of 'identification' and 'introjection' or 'internalization'. But the moral precepts that are internalized remain external to the individual's will, the super-ego remains dissociated from and hostile to the ego. What makes the individual heed these precepts is fear of his own aggression turned against himself. His moral responses are 'reaction-formations'. This is all of a piece with Freud's conception of morality as imposed on the individual and in conflict with his instinctive nature.

It remains true that Freud knows that internalization and identification cannot themselves create genuine autonomy. Although he talks of the ego as a servant of three harsh masters he recognizes the possibility of the ego making the demands of both the super-ego and the id its own and in the process transforming them: 'Where id was there ego shall be' — and similarly for the super-ego. This is developed in Melanie

Klein's writings. She makes it clear that while a strict super-
ego is indeed an aspect of the mind dissociated from the ego,
a genuine conscience is part of the ego. Still, just as Freud's
hedonistic conception of sexuality makes it difficult for him
to link sexuality with love, so his negative conception of
morality (morality as something imposed on the individual
and standing in his way) makes it difficult for him to think
of it as a constructive force in human life. His identification
of conscience and moral consciousness with the super-ego
makes him think of the demands of morality as intrinsically
incompatible with those of love and sexuality.

The conception of human nature that lies behind this is
bound up with the way he thinks of the relation between man
and the society in which he grows up. The discussion in the
chapter on 'Human Nature and Culture' calls this into question.
In *Civilization and its Discontents* Freud shows no recognition
of the extent to which man owes his humanity to the life
and culture in which he develops. I ask what might be meant
by saying that 'man is a social being' and I argue that there is
no suggestion here of anything being 'imposed' on the individual in the way Freud thought. I consider in what sense one
could say with truth that 'man is more than a beast' and even
that 'there is nevertheless a beast in man'. I argue that even if
there is some truth in Freud's claim, as I believe there is, that
as man becomes a moral and social being something in him
belonging to an earlier period is curbed and made subject to
control, it does not follow (i) that this is all there was to him
at the start (see Melanie Klein), nor (ii) that what he acquires
is not as much part of him, that what he becomes is not as
real as what is brought under check (see John Anderson). If
something that takes place here is best described in terms of
curbing and inhibition, much of what takes place soon goes
beyond this and is best described as growth and transformation. This is a central question raised by Freud's conception
of the development of the individual.

John Anderson has argued that on Freud's view nothing
new can enter into a man's life and become genuinely his,
and he has criticized this idea very powerfully. Indeed, this
idea is implicit in Freud's view that civilization is only a
veneer, that morality is alien to man's nature, that the ego is

at best a mediator between conflicting but external demands made on it by the id and the super-ego. It is explicitly stated by Freud in his comparison between the development of a village into a town and that of a child into a man, though not without some ambiguity. In the former case 'the old materials or forms have been superseded and replaced by new ones' and 'memory alone can trace the earlier features in the new image'. In the case of the mind 'every earlier stage of development persists alongside the later stage which has developed from it (Freud, 1950, vol. iv, p. 301). In my discussion of this comparison in an earlier chapter (see pp. 97—8) I suggest that there is truth in Freud's claim, though it is only a half-truth. What truth there is turns out to be a contingent one, whereas Anderson is concerned to criticize what is advanced as a necessary truth without being clearly recognized as such.

My own view is that while the view criticized by Anderson is certainly in Freud's writings, it is nevertheless true that Freud did recognize the difference between an individual who in his emotional development has progressed towards autonomy and one who has failed to do so. It is the latter he has in mind when he stresses how much what comes to the individual from outside remains external to his inner being, in conflict with it, and fails to transform it. As for the case where there is development towards relative autonomy, Freud emphasises something which Anderson neglects, namely what each man brings to what comes to him from outside in making it his own and how much this has a history which stretches back to his childhood.

When Freud said (1949c, p. 57) that 'men must be bound to one another libidinally' and that 'the advantages of common work would not hold them together,' Anderson retorted that 'man is not confronted with the task of living with his fellows' and that, being social, men 'are held together in common work' (Anderson, 1940, p. 347). This point, discussed in a different connection (pp. 78—80), is connected with the present one, for here too Anderson is stressing the reality of what belongs to a later stage of the individual's development. I argue that what Anderson emphasizes is perfectly true, but only because most men are on the whole co-operative, are interested in things, and pursue their interests in common activities. Anderson quite properly takes this for granted. If, on the other hand, men did not develop the ability to care and co-operate, living with their fellows would become a task and a problem. Freud does not take this for granted. He would agree with Malinowski that 'common sociability develops by extension of the family bonds' (Malinowski, 1955, p. 165), and he would say that in so far as those bonds are burdened with 'inner conflicts', men's ability to give and take, to co-operate with each other will be impaired. He thinks that love and the capacity to co-operate are intimately linked: 'love brings a change from egoism to altruism' (Freud, 1949c, p. 57).

It is clearly stated in Melanie Klein's writings that what is in question is something that appears very early in life and, if not thwarted, develops in the child's interaction with the outside world and in turn enables him to assimilate what he finds in such interaction. This process of growth, comprising many different forms of learning, involves a *transformation* of the child into an adult.

The antithesis of Freud's idea that culture is alien to man's nature is the idea that there is nothing to man other than what in him is the product of his culture. This idea too needs criticism, so in the final section of chapter 6 I ask whether it makes sense to talk of what man is like irrespective of the historical and cultural conditions in which men become individuals. I consider Malinowksi's positive and mature views in the fourth part of his book: 'Instinct and Culture'. I argue that it is difficult to keep clear of the picture of a raw material being turned into a finished product and that Malinowski does not entirely succeed in doing so. Still, he takes us some way towards a legitimate conception of human nature and I suggest that, alongside the view I have criticized, this legitimate conception can be extracted from Freud's writings. One could say that it is what has been distorted by the conceptual confusions I comment on, as well as by others.

In the last two chapters I am concerned with Freud's conceptions of emotional growth and maturity. I also consider the psycho-analytic view of character and its formation. I suggest that Freud was wrong to speak of 'the development of the libido' apart from 'the development of the ego'. This is connected with my earlier claim that a person's sexuality is both an expression of his personality and an important part of his perspective on the world. Thus development here involves learning. By this I mean emotional learning; in so far as this overlaps with moral learning, the discussion here is a continuation of the discussion of the two preceding chapters. I argue that Freud's real contribution here lies in his emphasis on the problematic character of individual development and the way it can be arrested by the individual's evasion of the problems he meets in the course of it. The growth towards autonomy and independence is thus a struggle with problems and difficulties in relationships with others — problems concerning the relinquishment of narcissism, hedonism, egotism and dependence. Indeed, the kind of development that is in question is the formation of the individual and his character, in the sense that as the individual struggles with difficulties he is contributing to his own growth and development. I argued earlier that Freud thought of the Oedipus situation, which the child helps to create around the ages of four to six, as constituting the most important of these difficulties. The Oedipus complex is the 'internal imprint' left by it. Until it is resolved it will reverberate in contemporary relationships and continue to attract attitudes belonging to the earlier situation. This is an instance of the form which an arrest takes in the context of the development of an individual.

In connection with character I consider Wilhelm Reich's views in his book *Character Analysis* and try to appreciate his insight as well as his limitations. Reich is mainly interested in weakness of character and the way a person's character can constitute resistance in a psycho-analysis. Developing Reich's ideas I suggest a classification of immature forms of character into reactive, impulsive, narcissistic and negative character traits. I conclude the last chapter with a discussion of the mature person and his character, and I make some tentative comments on the kind of connection there may be between moral goodness and emotional maturity.

Clearly my discussion of Freud is critical. But my main concern is to appreciate what he had to say. I write in the conviction that he was a great psychologist, the greatest of this century. Although the problems I discuss are philosophical problems, Freud himself was not primarily concerned with discussing philosophical difficulties. He was concerned with saying something about human beings, various aspects of their lives and some of the problems they meet there, in their relationships with each other. It is true that quite often philosophical presuppositions got in the way and distorted his insight. But this does not mean that this insight can no longer be discerned in what he said. Nor does it mean that it must be the reader's invention since 'it cannot have an existence apart from Freud's language'. I do not believe so, although I am familiar with arguments to the contrary. I believe, in fact, that clearing up the philosophical confusions in Freud's thinking can assist us in recovering his insight.

I say 'assist' since the clearing up of the philosophical confusions would not have this consequence by itself. We need to discern the spirit which informs Freud's concerns, and sometimes to read between the lines. But to do so is not to project or invent. It is to juxtapose Freud's own thoughts, expressed elsewhere, with the lines in question and to read the latter in the light of the former. It may even mean asking oneself: 'This is not what Freud would have wanted to say here, although it is what he does say. Had he recognized objections to it, or the way it conflicts with what he said elsewhere, how would he himself have taken forward the thought he was struggling to express?' To answer such a question is sometimes to 'reconstruct' Freud's thought and sometimes to 'develop' it — and the line between doing the one thing and doing the other is not a sharp one. On the whole I try to confine myself to the former and point out how others, especially Melanie Klein, have developed what is already in Freud's thinking.

I said that it is often possible to distinguish between the substance of Freud's thought and the way in which he expressed it, that is the form under which it appears in his writings; and I claimed that the former can be rescued from the philosophical presuppositions and conceptual confusions which shape the latter. Thus, to take an example, Freud had a penetrating perception of the extent to which people act in slavery to some part of themselves which they are unwilling to recognize. This can be gathered from the various things he wrote in connection with 'unconscious determination', 'repetition compulsion', 'resistance to analysis and change', 'the ego's slavery to the id and super-ego'. Clearly Freud devoted his efforts to developing a form of therapy which would reduce this slavery, free men from their bondage to the unconscious. Yet presuppositions regarding the scientific status of psychology and the lawfulness of the workings of the mind got him to subscribe to a form of determinism which made him think of the slavery he had perceived as an *inevitable* feature of human life: 'Are you asking me, gentlemen, to believe that there is anything which happens without a cause?' A philosopher who confined his attention to the familiar conceptual traps into which Freud fell in what he says might conclude that at least as far as his determinism goes, Freud had nothing to say.

Well, was he not a determinist then? He was. But his determinism was partly in the service of what he wanted to say independently of the philosophical presuppositions which bolster it up. True, what he had to say was distorted by these presuppositions; but not so distorted that it is no longer what it would be without the distortion and unrecognizable as such. I examine this particular question in *Freud's Conception of the Mind*.

Let me mention two further examples, relatively trivial though they happen to be. In his paper 'The Unconscious' Freud wrote (1950, vol. iv, p. 101): 'By the medium of consciousness each of us becomes aware only of his own state of mind.' Yet when his friend and colleague Fliess took him at his word Freud was annoyed (1954, letter 145): 'You take sides against me and tell me that "the thought-reader merely reads his own thoughts into other people", which deprives my work of all its value.' I say trivial since the above words are no more than a symptom of philosophical confusion. I suggested that this is not true of Freud's determinism. The second example comes from statements he made when attempting to justify the concept of the unconscious (Freud, 1980, vol. iv, pp. 99, 25). Thus he said, for instance, that 'consciousness yields no evidence' of what is unconscious and that we can only have 'indirect proofs' of it. Yet Freud explicitly stated that the psycho-analyst should aim at 'making the unconscious conscious'. He knew that the patient would resist facing his own unconscious mind and allowing its contents to become accessible to consciousness. He certainly did not think that this was an *impossibility*, however, as some of his conceptual reflections seemed to suggest to him.

Other examples could be cited. For instance, one could argue that Freud's early mechanistic and causal language is an anachronism, however much it may linger in some of his later statements, and that it stands in the way of a proper appreciation of his aims and achievements. One could argue that when he speaks of a 'dynamic theory of the mind' what is in question is the prominence which Freud gives to 'inner conflict', 'defence' and 'repression' in his study of the individual's emotional disturbances and behaviour. Central to this study are the individual's aims and motives which divide him in various ways, as Freud himself has explicitly stated when he said that 'all the categories which we employ to describe conscious mental acts, such as ideas, purposes, resolutions and so forth, can be applied to them,' i.e. to 'unconscious processes' (Freud, 1950, vol. iv, p. 101). Behind neurotic symptoms, he said, he was inclined to suspect 'the operation of intentions and purposes such as are to be observed in normal life' (Freud, 1948, p. 40).

Similarly I argue in this book that Freud's thinking on the character of man's motives and on the nature of his sexuality should not be identified with the hedonism which I criticize. The hedonism is there and so are the conceptual confusions which incline him to think of it as an inevitable feature of human life. But his real contribution lies in noticing a far-reaching reluctance in human life to give up certain positions prominent in early life which persist in the unconscious and to which we can regress in the face of certain difficulties — among these positions 'the quest for pleasure'. In his theoretical writings Freud referred to this as 'the pleasure principle' and contrasted it with a 'reality principle' of which he gave an extremely inadequate characterization.

Equally I suggest, although I argue this elsewhere (Dilman, forthcoming), that the divisions between the ego, the id and the super-ego are not absolute and immutable. They are only lines of demarcation which belong to Freud's method of representation. What Freud tried to highlight are genuine dissociations within the personality which can be healed. Thus while Freud spoke of the ego as a 'servant' in its relationship with the super-ego and the id, he did not mean to deny that it can achieve a position of mastery 'in its own house'. His contribution was to recognize that it cannot do so by sheer will-power and repression, but by putting its own house in order and by being prepared to give as well as take. This means the 'integration' of the dissociated aspects of the self, that is the person making his own the dissociated inclinations and alien precepts which, in turn, involves their modification.

I believe, in fact, that Freud had a keener perception than most who have been concerned with this topic of the dangers and pitfalls that lurk in the way of the realization of greater autonomy. Thus I argue in this book that Freud's near identification of conscience with the super-ego is in conflict with his own thinking on the subject, although philosophical confusions about the nature of morality prevent him from developing this thought. Similarly with regard to his conception of human nature. Here the tide in his own thoughts against which he has to swim in order to develop his insight regarding the relationship of the adult to the infant he was in the past is even greater. But I am anxious to see that this insight, which informs his conception of the development of the individual, is not lost in the face of criticism which many of the views in his later philosophical writings, especially *Civilization and its Discontents* and *The Future of an Illusion*, deserve. I do not think that these works should be read in isolation from Freud's other writings.

In short, then, in this book I am critical of an aspect of Freud's work in which certain trends of thinking are prominent. But, however deep-seated these trends may be, I do not believe that they represent what Freud really wanted to say. This is the distinctive position which I develop in this book. I hope to cover a wider area of Freud's contribution to psychology in my discussions, and I have already completed another book, *Freud's Conception of the Mind*, which discusses Freud's concept of the unconscious from the point of view of both knowledge and action, the ways in which Freud thought a person's past may determine his present, the prominence he gave to phantasy and the emotions in his account of human behaviour, the way in which he thought reason and emotion enter into human actions, his ideas of repression and the divisions of the personality, his conception of self-knowledge, and his views on freedom and determinism. I hope to complete this discussion with a book which examines his conception of psycho-therapy — *Insight and Therapy*.

1

Sexuality and the Child

1 Freud's Conceptual Treatment of Sexuality

Since the early days of psycho-analysis Freud's concern to treat and understand neuroses led him, in different ways, to the subject of sexuality. Professional associates first put the idea into his mind: Breuer, Charcot, and the gynaecologist Dr Chrobak (Freud, 1950, vol. i, pp. 294–6). The first suggestions about the sexual aetiology of neuroses were crude and they led Freud to connect the so-called 'actual neuroses' with sexual frustration and anxiety.

Freud later came upon sexuality in connection with the 'psycho-neuroses' in a different way, namely in the 'associations' of his patients. These associations led to events in the past in which the patient remembered being the witness or victim of other people's sexuality. Freud tried to connect the neurotic symptoms he was treating with the emotionally disturbing effect of these early experiences. The disappearance of the symptom or the amelioration of the patient's condition upon the recollection of these events in their emotional vividness led Freud to make the connection.

When later he was forced to recognize that the events in question had not occurred and were a figment of the patient's imagination, there were two alternatives open to him: either they were recent phantasies, put into the patient's mind by Freud himself and projected into the past, or they were phantasies which the patient indulged in at the time. Freud rejected the first alternative and so concluded that the patient, as a child, had been sexually active in imagination. This meant that the child must have had sexual desires. His consideration of 'sexual aberrations' in his *Three Essays on the Theory of Sexuality* (first published in 1905) is an attempt to provide a philosophical foundation for this belief.[1]

In fact the *Three Essays* constitute Freud's most systematic treatment of the question 'What is sexuality, if it can be said to characterize human life from its very beginning?' In the first essay, 'The Sexual Aberrations', he is concerned with the different ways in which sex enters into various phenomena — inversions and perversions, infatuation, sadism and masochism, and neurotic symptoms. In what sense are these phenomena of sexuality? If we can represent them as such what light, in each case, does this throw on our concept of sexuality? In his treatment of these questions Freud evolves a conceptual apparatus in terms of which he attempts to exhibit their relations to ordinary adult sexuality, as well as to each other. In the second essay, 'Infantile Sexuality', he puts forward arguments in favour of infantile sexuality. These rely on the conceptual framework he has developed in the first essay for the connections they aim to establish. In the last part of this essay, 'The Phases of Development of the Sexual Organisation', and in the third essay, 'The Transformations of Puberty', Freud sketches an account of the development of human sexuality and the way it changes character in the course of the individual's physical and emotional growth.

I begin with Freud's analysis of sexuality as something that has diverse manifestations in human life and is capable of growth in the course of the individual's life. He asks in what sense the various 'aberrations' he examines are phenomena of sexuality. He proceeds by exploring analogies, forging connections, and developing a mode of presentation in which these connections will appear as natural. His concern throughout is to do justice to the different things we regard as belonging to sexuality. He argues against the idea that the act of copulation needs to be the central point of a person's sexuality and warns us 'to loosen the bond that exists in our thoughts

---

[1] Philosophically Freud's 'justification of the idea of infantile sexuality' belongs with his 'justification for the conception of the unconscious'. All quotations from *Three Essays* are taken from the 1949 English edition.

between the sexual instinct and the sexual object' (Freud, 1949a, p. 26).

He refers to sexuality as an 'instinct' and speaks of its 'aim' and 'object'. He notes that in its manifestations it permits wide variations in both respects. This is what he calls its 'plasticity'. The 'aim' is what it seeks. In this respect Freud thinks of sexuality as impersonal, belonging with that aspect of the individual's mind Freud calls the 'id'. Here the individual is a vehicle through which his sexuality works, although the form in which it finds expression is an important aspect of his character. Freud sees the 'aim' of sexuality as being to obtain pleasure through the stimulation of those parts of the body he calls 'erotogenic zones'.

He thinks of the urge towards these particular forms of pleasure as distinct impulses and refers to them as the 'components of the sexual instinct'. They belong to or constitute its 'sensual current'. He says: 'The sexual instinct itself may be no simple thing, but put together from components which have come apart in the perversions' (p. 41). In fact, he characterizes perversions as sexual activities in which sexuality deviates from its 'normal aim', namely the union of the genitals in the act of copulation (p. 28). The individual is driven towards the particular aim which his sexuality assumes much in the way that a man is driven to seek food by hunger (see Freud, 1949b, p. 263). Freud speaks of what thus drives him as 'the energy of the sexual instinct' and he calls it 'libido'.

All this constitutes one aspect of human sexuality. The other aspect is its object-directed character. Here Freud speaks of the individual's 'object-choice'. Under this aspect human sexuality is not something impersonal: Freud sees it as constituting one basis of the individual's attachments to other people. Just as the erotogenic aspect constitutes its 'sensual current', this aspect constitutes its 'affectionate current'. The individual's 'object-choice' and the form it takes is for Freud the most important dimension of what he calls 'the development of the ego', in other words the individual's development towards greater autonomy.

Freud claims that at its earliest stage the infant's sexuality is 'auto-erotic', in other words not 'object-seeking'. This is followed by a 'narcissistic' stage when the child becomes the object of his own sexuality — 'primary narcissism'. Soon, however, the child's parents and those who look after him or her become the object of his or her sexuality, the child's particular object-choice and sexual attitude being determined by its gender. At this stage this attitude varies between 'activity' and 'passivity'. Freud says that we are inclined 'to dispute the possibility of identifying a child's affection. . .for those who look after him with sexual love' (Freud, 1949a, p. 100). He goes on to argue that a closer examination would show this to be a prejudice: 'A child's intercourse with anyone responsible for his care affords him an unending source of sexual excitation and satisfaction from his erotogenic zones' (p. 100).

Here Freud speaks of the Oedipus complex and he says that it is 'the peak of infantile sexuality'. 'It exercises a decisive influence on the sexuality of adults. . .Every object-choice whatever is based, though less closely, on these [early] prototypes' (pp. 104–6). When the child reaches the age of puberty, if he is to be able to develop towards greater autonomy he or she has to detach himself sexually from the parent of the opposite sex and outgrow his or her feelings of rivalry with the parent of the same sex.

There are other complexities here, however, which may lead to 'inversions' and other forms of 'sexual aberration'. Freud had characterized perversions in terms of deviations from what is regarded as the 'normal' *aim* of sexuality. Similarly he characterizes perversions in terms of deviations from what is regarded as the 'normal' *object* of sexuality, namely an adult of the opposite sex not a parent, brother or sister. However, in his comparisons Freud treats ordinary adult sexuality more as a methodological point of reference than a norm. He says (1949b, p. 271): 'There is no difference between perverse and normal sexuality. . .In one case one ruling family has usurped all the power, in the other, another.' The fact remains that he regards 'genital organisation' as a more mature form of sexuality and that what he means by 'maturity' cannot be given solely in chronological terms.

'Perversions', then, are attenuated forms of sexuality. In them a person's sexuality does not centre around the genitals and does not serve the aim of procreation. The activities that constitute perversions are forms of sexuality in that they do often lead to orgasm, are regarded by the person himself as sexual in character, and enter into and play a part in ordinary adult sexual intercourse. Freud could have added that we find a knowledge of these connections in pornographic literature, in sexual jokes and insults.

In his account of 'infatuation' Freud takes a similar line to the one he took in his account of perversions. 'Perversions,' he said, 'are sexual activities which either (a) extend, in an anatomical sense, beyond the regions of the body that are designed for sexual union, or (b) linger over the immediate relations to the sexual object which should normally be traversed rapidly on the path towards the final sexual aim' (Freud, 1949a, p. 28). In infatuation, too, 'the goal of the sexual instinct' does not stop short at the genitals. 'The appreciation extends to the whole body of the sexual object. . .and spreads over into the psychological sphere' (p. 29). Freud sees part of what is involved here under the aspect of 'fetishism'. I am thinking of the way certain features of the beloved, such as some blemish of the face, a lisp, or some peculiarity of mannerism, may dominate the aspect under which she is seen and make a vital contribution to her spell over the lover. The peculiarity in question is seen as the expression of something which touches a soft spot in the lover or poses a challenge to which he rises. The quality of his feelings and the permanance of his attachment will then depend on what it is that is touched in him, protectiveness, for instance, or the desire to possess. It will depend on what else there is in the beloved to sustain or transform his response, and what else there is in the lover to enable him to integrate it so that his infatuation can turn into love.

Though he was later to change his view, in the *Three Essays* Freud treats 'sadism' as a kind of perversion, without calling it that: 'Sadism would correspond to an aggressive component of the sexual instinct which has become independent and exaggerated and, by displacement, has usurped the leading position' (p. 36). What is displaced here is affection or tenderness, although Freud does not say so explicitly. Free from their influence, this component turns into cruelty and is enjoyed sexually in its own right. What thus turns into cruelty is the 'aggressiveness' which Freud speaks of as 'an element' contained in 'the sexuality of most male human beings' (p. 36).

What he has in mind, I think, is the thrusting form of determination on the part of the male to pursue the female of his choice, to overcome obstacles that stand in his way, to fight over her, to rouse and take her in the sexual act. It is the assertiveness that characterizes male sexuality and which Freud opposes to passivity. It does not, of course, exclude tenderness and protectiveness. It turns into the kind of cruelty that characterises sadism in the absence of such tenderness. I doubt, however, whether it can be properly characterized as a 'component' of sexuality, since what is in question is one of the *forms* which the expression of sexuality takes both under its sensual and its affectionate aspects. For what we are dealing with is the way in which the personality of the subject enters into relationship with the opposite sex and determines what expression his sexuality takes there.

I am suggesting that what Freud sees as a characteristic of male sexuality may be a feature of a person's character of either gender rather than one specifically of the male libido. If that were so, the connection between sadism and sexuality would have to be made differently from the way Freud makes it in the *Three Essays*. It would not be possible to represent it as a distortion of what belongs to male sexuality exclusively.

In the *Three Essays* 'masochism' is thought of as inverted sadism, sadism directed to oneself — in the way that 'narcissim' is thought of as love directed to oneself — except that in 'primary narcissism' there is no inversion of love (see Freud, 1950, vol. iv). That is, masochism is thought of as a secondary phenomenon. Later Freud was to regard it as a primary phenomenon and subordinate it to the 'death instinct', treating sadism as a derivative of it.

So sadistic cruelty, in Freud's view, is the expression of something that belongs to sex, though it is distorted in its isolation from the affectionate aspect of sex. This latter aspect may not have had the chance to develop or it may be repressed. A person may not be capable of tenderness and may have to learn much before he can have tender feelings towards others, or he may not allow himself to feel and show tenderness towards any person, especially members of the opposite sex. Freud does not go into this in his *Three Essays*, but he obviously regards it as the kind of condition which encourages the development of sadism, particularly when a man has a chip on his shoulder about the opposite sex. However, with this introduction of a retaliatory element we move away from the cases Freud had in mind, for with it the cruelty in question is subordinated to revenge and is not enjoyed for its own sake. Revenge is not a form of sexuality even when it exploits sex and is directed against a 'crime' which belongs to sex.

In Freud's view sexual 'impotence' is in some ways the reverse of sadism, though he does not say so. For in sadism it is the 'aggressive element' that displaces affection and tenderness, usurps the leading position and is distorted into cruelty. In impotence it is this 'aggressive element' that is repressed, leaving the affectionate and tender aspect of a man's sexuality isolated and, therefore, lame.[2] I said that sexual impotence is 'in some ways' the reverse of sadism. This qualification is necessary since sadism is considered to be an expression of sexuality, whereas impotence is a failure to give it expression. Besides, the idea of tenderness usurping a leading position is almost a contradiction in terms. What we have here, in Freud's view, is tenderness without the support of sensuality, a form of tenderness that lacks confidence in its own capacity to give and to sustain.

The female counterpart of impotence is frigidity. Freud comments on this in the short section entitled 'The Differentiation between Men and Women'. His view is that the distinction between the masculine and femine characters is not established until puberty: 'The auto-erotic activity of the erotogenic zones is the same in both sexes. . .The sexuality of little girls is of a wholly masculine character' (p. 96). During puberty clitoridal sexuality, which Freud characterizes as 'a piece of masculine sexuality', is overtaken by repression. After a lapse of time 'during which the young woman is anaesthetic', erotogenic susceptibility to stimulation is 'transferred from the clitoris

[2] Freud discusses this matter in the second of his 'Three Contributions to the Psychology of Love' – 1910, 1912, 1918. See Freud, 1950, vol. iv.

to the vaginal orifice'. The woman 'adopts a new leading zone for the purposes of her later sexuality' (pp. 98—9). If, however, during the period when this transference takes place, 'the clitoridal zone refuses to abandon its excitability,' the temporary anaesthesia becomes permanent. Freud says that the inability to make this transition from one zone to the other is 'an event for which the way is prepared by an extensive activity of the clitoridal zone in childhood' (p. 98). Freud makes clear that what he is describing here are 'the erotogenic determinants of anaesthesia' and not its 'psychic determinants'.

We see that Freud is arguing that sexuality enters into and pervades a greater area of human life than we recognize. At the same time, and as the other side of the coin, he argues that what we find in these diverse areas of human life *are* manifestations of sexuality. We are justified in characterizing them as manifestations of 'sexuality' in a sense of that term catered for by its accepted meaning. Freud believed that common prejudice restricts the application of the term sanctioned by its accepted sense. He saw himself as making explicit this sense of which we have in some ways lost recognition. This can be characterized as a 'conceptual analysis'. Freud carries out such an analysis through a series of comparisons, the co-ordinates of which are determined by 'the conceptual scaffolding' which he sets up to deal with 'the psychic manifestations of sexual life', in other words to be able to represent them as manifestations of sexuality (p. 94).

He arranges the phenomena in question in a 'connected series', held together by 'indirect' connections which he exhibits by presenting 'intermediate examples' (p. 16). The following are some of the prominent links which Freud indicates: (a) 'Here are factors which provide a point of contact between the perversions and normal sexual life and which can also serve as a basis for their classification' (p.28). We have seen what they are. (b) 'Symptoms are formed in part at the cost of abnormal sexuality; neuroses are, so to say, the negative of perversions' (p.44). (c) 'Perverted sexuality is nothing else but infantile sexuality, magnified and separated into its component parts' (1949b, p. 261).

Some of the phenomena in question are thus represented

as attenuated forms of 'normal adult sexuality', deviating from it in various respects. They lack some of the features which we may be inclined to regard as essential to human sexuality. Freud argues that the kind of unity we find in 'normal' sexuality is fragile and can become fragmented along different axes. It can vary in its 'aim' according to which component erotogenic impulse dominates in its organization. It may lose its aim altogether when its 'sensual current' becomes dissociated from its 'affectionate current' and repressed. Here Freud speaks of 'aim-inhibited love'. Or it may lose its 'object' and turn into a craving for erotogenic pleasure, as in some perversions. All this makes Freud wonder whether there is anything 'essential and constant in the sexual instinct' (1949a, p. 36).

Thus in his analysis of sexuality Freud discusses both the erotogenic aspect of sexuality and its object-directedness. But he does not say much about affection and he leaves one with the impression that he regards the quest for pleasure as central to sexuality. He does not sufficiently emphasize the 'transcendent' aspect of sexuality prominent in affection, by which I mean the aspect of sexuality in which pleasure is found in the giving of it and where this pleasure is not an aim but a by-product. I shall return to this question in the last section of this chapter.

2 Freud's Argument for Infantile Sexuality

Freud regards the 'popular view that the sexual instinct is absent in childhood and only awakens in puberty' as a common prejudice which he attributes to 'infantile amnesia': 'the peculiar amnesia which, in the case of most people. . .hides the earliest beginnings of their childhood up to their sixth or eighth year' (Freud, 1949a, pp. 51–2). As he puts it in his *Introductory Lectures* (1949b, p. 262): 'What does actually awake in them at this period is the reproductive function, which then makes use for its own purposes of material lying to hand in body and mind.'

What Freud refers to as 'material lying to hand' are the cravings for erotogenic pleasure which the adolescent boy has experienced as a child. Thus, attracted to a girl of his own age, he will want to hug, kiss, embrace and fondle her, all of these familiar to him in his relationship with his mother. If he gives in, he will find the transition to fondling and caressing the breasts, thighs and genitals of the girl at once natural and fear-provoking — the fear of transgression. Freud characterizes this as the fear of the incest-barrier, to which I shall return in the following chapter. The day-dreams in which the adolescent's feelings thrive have aspects continuous with thoughts and phantasies that date back to earlier periods of his life, centring around his mother, sisters and other women — women real or imaginary, invested with roles and qualities of his mother, pictured as attending to his bodily needs, feeding and bathing him, playing with him, looking after him. Nowhere is it more visible than at this transitionary stage how much adult sexual life, desires, conflicts and experiences are 'rooted in' infantile life and phantasies, grow out of them, and feed on them. Freud says (1949b, p. 262) that the supposition that 'children should have no sexual life — sexual excitement, needs and gratification of a sort — but that they should suddenly acquire these things in the years between twelve and fourteen. . .[is] biologically just as improbable, indeed, nonsensical, as to suppose that they are born without genital organs which first begin to sprout at the age of puberty'.

He points out that many of those who deny sexuality in children contradict themselves and betray their recognition of it in different ways — for instance by being 'the last to relax educative measures against it' (Freud, 1949b, p. 263). In the first part of *Sex and Repression in Savage Society*, where he is more sympathetic to Freud on this question than in the later parts, Malinowski writes that 'a well-known piece of advice given by old gossips to young mothers in peasant communities is to the effect that boys about the age of three should sleep separately from the mother'. He continues: 'The occurrence of infantile erections is well known in these communities, as is also the fact that the boy clings to the mother in a different way from a girl' (Malinowski, 1955, p. 42).

In a passage worth quoting from his *Introductory Lectures*, Freud makes the same point (1949b, pp. 279—80):

It is easy to see that the little man wants his mother all to himself, finds his father in the way, becomes restive when the latter takes upon himself to caress her, and shows his satisfaction when the father goes away or is absent. He often expresses his feelings directly in words and promises his mother to marry her...One might try to object that the little boy's behaviour is due to egoistic motives and does not justify the conception of an erotic complex; the mother looks after all the child's needs and consequently it is to the child's interest that she should trouble herself about no one else. This too is quite correct; but it is soon clear that in this, as in similar dependent situations, egoistic interests only provide the occasion on which the erotic impulses seize. When the little boy shows the most open sexual curiosity about his mother, wants to sleep with her at night, insists on being in the room while she is dressing, or even attempts physical acts of seduction, as the mother so often observes and laughingly relates, the erotic nature of this attachment to her is established without a doubt. Moreover, it should not be forgotten that a mother looks after a little daughter's needs in the same way without producing this effect; and that often enough a father eagerly vies with her in trouble for the boy without succeeding in winning the same importance in his eyes as the mother. In short, the factor of sex preference is not to be eliminated from the situation by any criticisms.

Freud represents infantile sexual life as having two aspects. On the one hand there are the bodily pleasures at first openly but soon after illicitly sought and enjoyed, pleasures that form the centre of phantasies and come to be characterized by the phantasies themselves. Freud mentions thumb-sucking, interest in producing and retaining stools, and also infantile masturbation. On the other hand there is the relational, give-and-take aspect, which is at first wholly directed to the mother or mother-substitutes. In auto-erotism the child or infant seeks pleasure through his own body. These pleasures, however, soon come to be characterized by phantasies which, in however rudimentary a form, bring in a reference to other persons. Thus another person may be brought into the activity as a condition of the pleasure obtained, if only as an onlooker and in phantasy. Freud points out that even if auto-erotism is at first dominant, reference to another person is not altogether absent. Gradually it begins to play a growing part. But in the *Three Essays* he puts greater stress on the erotogenic aspect and does not do enough to bring out how this aspect may characterize the infant's relationship with his mother and how it is, in turn, characterized by the form of that relationship. This is a deficiency which is remedied in the work of Melanie Klein and her followers.

Freud's argument for infantile sexuality largely centres on this emphasis on the erotogenic aspect of the infant's bodily functions, activities and experiences, and on the way he connects them with adult perversions. Having connected perversions with adult sexuality, he next proceeds to relate these perversions to infantile sexuality. Freud's reasons for characterizing certain infantile activities centring round various bodily organs as 'sexual' — as in the case of thumb-sucking which he directly connects with sucking the breast — are as follows:

1 The analogy between the preparatory actions to adult sexual intercourse and the consummatory actions of the infantile impulse.

2 The pleasure obtained and later sought independently of the vital function of the organ in question — independently of nutrition, as in thumb-sucking: 'The behaviour of a child who indulges in thumb-sucking is determined by a search for some pleasure which has already been experienced and is now remembered' (Freud, 1949a, p. 60).

3 The analogy between the immediate after-effects of e.g. sucking of the breast and those of adult intercourse: 'Sensual sucking involves a complete absorption of the attention and leads either to sleep or even to a motor reaction in the nature of an orgasm. It is not infrequently combined with rubbing some sensitive part of the body such as the breast or the external genitalia. Many children proceed by this path from sucking to masturbation' (Freud, 1949a, pp. 58–9).

4 The way these different aspects are integrated into adult sexuality and can become detached in the perversions. They precede adult sexuality, are taken into it, and are transferred in the process, although they may resist transformation.

3 Some Weaknesses in the Argument

What Freud's argument attempts to establish is to the point, although it is not enough, and some of his reasons for his conclusion are weak as they stand. These two points are interconnected. Take first the analogy between the infantile and childish acts and those that belong to the preparatory stage of adult sexual intercourse. It is not enough to establish the sexual character of the childish acts. After all, even if they can be shown to express something that is partly identical in the two situations, e.g. love in some of the caresses or anger in biting, there will be the further problem of showing that the love or anger is necessarily an expression of sexuality. And this can be reasonably contested — they may be the expressions of the lover's personality in adult sexuality which date back to early childhood. But it does not follow that their early expressions in childhood have to be characterized as sexual.

Take next 'organ pleasure' which Freud describes as 'erotogenic'. The mere fact that pleasure is sought and obtained does not establish the presence of sexuality. Malinowski raises a similar objection (1955, p. 42):

> The relation between an infant and its mother is essentially different from a sexual attitude. Instincts must be defined not simply by introspective methods, not merely by analysis of the feeling tones such as pain and pleasure, but above all by their function. . . The relation of the suckling to its mother is first of all induced by the desire for nutrition. The bodily clinging of a child to its mother again satisfies its bodily wants of warmth, protection and guidance. The child is not fit to cope with the environment by its own forces alone, and as the only medium through which it can act is the maternal organism it clings instinctively to the mother. In sexual relations the aim of bodily attraction and clinging is the union which leads to impregnation. Each of these two innate tendencies. . .covers a big range of preparatory and consummatory actions which present certain similarities. The line of division, however, is clear, because one set of acts. . .serves to complete the infant's unripe organism. . .the other set of acts subserves the union of sexual organs and the production of a new individual.

Freud knew that the relation of the suckling to its mother is in the first place induced by the desire for nutrition (Freud, 1949a, p. 60), and he argued convincingly against the 'essentialism' and 'functionalism' (Darwinian) which appears in the passage. However, Malinowski goes on to raise a serious objection which Freud needs to answer (p. 212):

> We cannot. . .accept the simple solution that the temptation of
> incest is due to sexual relation between the infant and mother.
> The sensuous pleasure which is common to both relations is a
> component of every successful instinctive behaviour. The pleasure
> index cannot serve to differentiate instincts, since it is a general
> character of them all.

Malinowski does not deny the existence of incestuous
tendencies: 'under the mechanisms which constitute the human
family serious temptations to incest arise' (p. 211). But he
claims that these tendencies do not belong to childhood;
they arise at the time of adolescence and with the onset of
puberty: 'the subconscious temptation to incest arises from
the blending of early memories with new experience' (p. 214);
'the retrospective power of new sentiments in man is the
cause of incestuous temptations' (p. 215). If by 'incest' is
understood 'adult sexual intercourse with the mother', then
Freud is in agreement with Malinowski. What Malinowski
calls 'mechanism of sentiment formation' Freud describes as
'retrogressive phantasy-making' (1949b, p. 282): 'We dis-
cover. . .that the sexual desires towards the mother have been
moulded into forms which would have been as yet foreign to
the child.' But he claims that it would be a vain attempt to
explain the whole of the son's sexual attraction for his mother
by 'retrogressive phantasy-making'. The sexual character of
that attraction comes in part from the period before puberty.

Malinowski puts the difference between Freud's view and
his own as follows (1955, p. 214): 'Freud assumes a continuous persistence from infancy of the same attitude towards
the mother. In our argument we try to show that there is
only a partial identity between the early and the later drives,
that this identity is due essentially to the mechanism of sentiment formation.' But the assumption of 'a continuous persistence of the same attitude' does not imply anything more
than 'a partial identity'. For while the identity on which
Freud insisted is in respect of the sexual character of the
attitudes towards the mother, he clearly did not think that
what gives an attitude its sexual character is always the same

thing. This is the big difference between Freud and Malinowski here. In his early observations Malinowski recognized 'infantile sexuality' in an imaginative way (1955, chapter 5). Later, however, he restricts the use of the term 'sexual' in the way that Freud opposed.

All the same there is in what Malinowski says in the passage quoted above a justified criticism of one of Freud's reasons for characterizing the infantile activities in question as sexual. The sensuous pleasure common to these activities and 'the preparatory actions of the sexual drive' cannot give them an exclusive connection, since it is 'a component of every successful instinctive behaviour'. Indeed, if the sensuous pleasure in the 'erotogenic' activities of the infant is sexual, it is so because of the infant's or child's attitude towards these activities, his parents' and other people's attitude to him as the agent of these activities, and the phantasies with which he surrounds them. Obviously the earlier one goes back in the child's life the more difficult it is to attribute to him the required thoughts and phantasies. Surely it would not be a serious retraction if Freud were to admit that sexuality makes its appearance gradually, though its beginnings can be detected early in the child's life.

This point is in fact made by Malinowski in the early part of his book (1955, p. 41) in connection with what Freud calls 'anal erotism': 'From an age of about four to six years, the "indecent" centres round interests in excretory functions, exhibitionism and games with indecent exposure, often associated with cruelty.' Malinowski is referring to European children and he makes it clear that in Melanesia he has failed to find 'any traces of what could be called infantile indecencies, or of a subterranean world in which children indulge in clandestine pastimes centring round excretory functions or exhibitionism'. There, he says, 'we find an altogether different type of sexual development in the child' (p. 43). He goes on to point out that 'the category of "indecent" is created by elders,' (p. 54) and that 'the "indecency" which among bourgeois children is fostered by the repression of the natural curiosities is much less pronounced in the lower classes.' (p. 55).

Frowning, disapproval, shaming, the threat of punishment

on the part of adults constitute *one* of the set of attitudes
that condition the way the child comes to regard certain
natural activities, the way he extends them in certain directions, and the way he surrounds them with certain phantasies.
Whether or not they succeed in stopping these activities in
particular cases, they greatly contribute to the fascination
they exert on the child, to the magnetic quality of their
attraction. This is bound up with the way they come to be
severed from what is matter-of-fact in daily life. It is not so
much the sensuous, bodily pleasures as such which connect
such activities as sucking the breast or thumb, retaining stools,
or masturbating the penis, with 'the sexual', as the emotions,
the peculiar excitement with which they are invested. This is
sexuality, as we find it in the life of the child, and it has
nothing to do with genital procreation. In fact, it is the
phantasies which genital procreation is capable of attracting
which account for some of its magic. I said 'sexuality' in the
life of the child such as we may find it in isolated moments
when it is not disturbed by fear. It is with reference to this
that its attenuated expressions can be recognized. The pleasures which Freud referred to in his argument for infantile
sexuality are not purely physical, and they do not constitute
'a component of every successful instinctive behaviour'. As
Malinowski knows well, the way in which the child *thinks* of
what he is doing characterizes the pleasure which he seeks
and may experience. That is why the instinctive aspect, as he
himself brings out so well, is only one aspect of human
sexuality in contrast with animals.

Sexuality is a plant that grows in two very different envir-
onments: in the dark and in the accepting intimacy of a
personal relationship. Both exclude the light that defuses
sexuality; this is their connecting link. The intimacy of the
relationship between mother and child, its exclusiveness,
has the possibility of providing the right kind of environment
for the growth of the child's sexuality. Once more the purely
physical aspect of the contact between mother and child is
not sufficient to explain the sexual character which Freud
attributes to the relationship. We have to ask what goes into
this intimacy besides the physical contact. We have to take
into account the way the mother regards her child, the

significance she attributes to the relationship and what she tries to make of it. I do not mean only consciously, but unconsciously as well. This is what the child responds to, not just the oral pleasure of sucking the breast. There is interaction between mother and child and the flow of pleasure is not one-way.

The child responds to his mother as a person; he responds to the love, possessiveness and narcissism she puts into the way she cares for him. It is clear to me that almost from the beginning he responds to her emotions and changes of mood, at least in the sense that he is affected by them, that they register in his behaviour, e.g. during feeding. Dr Winnicott gives a very sensitive account of this in the first part of his book *The Child and the Family*. He writes of how, by allowing the baby to play in her arms and at her breast, the mother will see his excitement in its proper proportions and recognize it as a form of love (Winnicott, 1957, p. 11). He writes of how the baby can be scared of his own feelings and how he can be helped 'by allowing play, by allowing him to mouth the nipple, perhaps to handle it; anything that the infant can let himself enjoy, till at last he gains the confidence to take the risk and suck' (p. 11). He brings out how much the feeding and caring of the baby is a give-and-take, using the example of an older ten-month-old baby whose attention is attracted by a silver spoon lying on the table. He wants to grasp it, but at first he is hesitant. When a look at his mother reassures him that he has her approval, he grabs it. He soon (Winnicott, 1957, p. 34)

> discovers what he wants to do with it, because his mouth begins to get excited. . .Saliva begins to flow from his mouth. . .His mouth begins to want the spoon. His gums begin to want to enjoy biting on it. It is not very long before he has put it in his mouth. Then he has feelings about it in the ordinary aggressive way that belongs to lions and tigers, and babies, when they get hold of something good. He makes as if to eat it. We can now say that the baby has taken this thing and made it his own. . .I would say that in imagination he has eaten it.

Winnicott speaks of this as a 'game', an 'exercise of the imagination'. He sees it as an expression of the 'imaginative life of the infant, which enriches and is enriched by the bodily experience' (p. 37).

What does he mean by 'imagination' and 'imaginative' in this context? I think he means that the activities in question involve *play* which gives them a significance that goes beyond their character as feeding. This element of play that is clearly visible in the case of the baby with the spoon is not absent in the actual feeding situation. Winnicott relates them very closely. The baby approaches and responds to all expressions of his mother's love as she ministers to his bodily needs in the way that he responds to food and vice versa. He treats it all as something to be incorporated and made his own. This is an instance of what Melanie Klein describes as a phantasy — one that gives content to what she calls 'introjection'. The infant cannot obviously as yet think of what he is doing in separation from his actions — he has no language — and his phantasies lie in the way he treats the spoon or the mother's breast. The significance it has for him can be seen in his behaviour, but it is not something which he can bring before his mind or contemplate. This is the connection between play and imagination here; the connection is an internal one.

So far I have suggested the way we can connect the young infant's response to his mother at her breast with love. But does this mean that the pleasure he finds in sucking the breast can be characterized as 'sexual'? This would depend on our willingness to characterize the love he enjoys at the breast as 'sexual'. Well, it is a love that finds expression in bodily contact, craves this contact and finds completion in it. It is a love which treats this bodily contact as a form of union with the mother. The pleasure which the baby finds at the breast is the enjoyment of this union. The gratification it gives the baby involves the experience of giving up all exertion and activity which, later if not just as yet, are an embodiment of the will. In this letting go of the will we have a precursor of later forms of sexual orgasm. Still one must remember that if one is willing to talk of sexuality here one is referring to elementary forms of it.

So much for the first year or year and a half of the child's life. As he grows up and learns to speak, gains greater autonomy and separateness from his mother, and becomes exposed to a wider range of attitudes from others, much that is *new* will enter into his life and phantasies. There will be a forward movement in his life connected with new interests. But there will also be a harking back to his earlier intimacy with his mother, which he is now capable of imaginatively investing with a new significance. He will be able to think of it in terms which he was incapable of comprehending earlier. This is what Freud calls 'retrogressive phantasy-making'. However, he will find a great deal in the attitudes of those around him that discourages this tendency, and he will consequently check it and deny the inclination. Freud's claim is that it will nevertheless remain with him and at a later stage constitute one of the components of what he calls the Oedipus complex.

4 Deficiencies in Freud's Conceptual Framework

Freud's analysis of the sexual instinct into various components reminds me of Hume's analysis of the emotions. It represents complex conceptual relations as mere contingent contiguities between elements which can be understood in isolation from each other and from the surroundings in which they can be seen as related. The 'components' on which Freud focuses are in fact the forms which the individual's sexuality takes. In the abstract they can be spoken of as different aspects of sexuality. We can see them as such, however, only in the light of our understanding of what sexuality is — we cannot build up that understanding piecemeal by a consideration of each aspect in turn. Freud shows some recognition of this in the way he tries to relate them to what we regard as central to sexuality. So his arguments take our concept of sexuality for granted; they could not get going at all unless this was so. What I say may appear paradoxical in view of Freud's belief that our conception of sexuality is too narrow, but the paradox is resolved if we admit the possibility of a discrepancy between what we *say* we mean when we speak of sexuality and what the word actually means in the language we speak when taken in its many connections. Freud believed that while the restriction in our understanding reflects certain 'common prejudices', there are strands in our ordinary use of the word which give the lie to these prejudices. So he speaks of his recommended extensions as 'restorations' rather than 'innovations'.[3]

While we share Descartes' inclination to identify the mental with consciousness and this inclination has its source in our language, nevertheless our ordinary concept of mind, when understood properly, does allow the possibility of talking intelligibly of unconscious states of mind. Likewise we are inclined to confine our use of the term 'sex' to activities that centre around the genitals and relate to reproduction.[4] This inclination is not just an expression of narrow-mindedness; it comes from something important in what we mean by the word. It would be a mistake to treat it lightly. Nevertheless, if we gave way to it we would be ignoring the richness of this meaning, and Freud was right to oppose it.

I objected to Freud's notion of sexuality as made up of 'components'. I said that 'aggressiveness' and 'cruelty', for instance, are not components of sexuality but aspects of a person's character as shown in his sexuality. This sexuality, in turn, may be said to be one of the fundamental modes of his relationships with others and of the pleasure he finds in these relationships. He enters into them as a person with individual characteristics, but the mode which constitutes the sexual character of what he gives and takes, does and experiences, can be characterized without reference to the individual. This is like characterizing features of a language, such as the meanings of words in English, without reference to the speakers who use these words to say what they want to say — although if there were no speakers there would be no words to have any meaning.

In fact we could speak of sexuality as a 'grammar' of personal contact and relationship, and equally of 'the language of sex'. Certainly if we wish to become clear about what human sexuality involves we cannot ignore the language of sex. Human sexuality, like human thought, evolves in the life of each individual and changes with it. In the context of a person's early relationships and the beginnings of thought

---

[3] Freud, 1948, p. 68. See also Freud, 1949b, p. 268.
[4] Freud himself notes this parallel. See Freud, 1949b, p. 268.

and speech it is bound to be different from what it is like in adult life. Freud's distinctive contribution was to represent it as the precursor of adult sexuality and as such partaking of some of its character. He further argued that residues of it survive the development of the individual and may be found in adult sexuality — in overt form in perversions and in covert form in neurotic symptoms. Hence the place which an examination of aberrant sexuality occupies in Freud's study of sex in the *Three Essays*.

I have criticized Freud's notion of 'components of the sex instinct' for obscuring the way in which a person enters into aspects of his sexuality as an individual. All the same it has the virtue of bringing into prominence the possibility of the fragmentation of sexual life. A person's sexuality may be one-sided and even take on a grotesque form because what he puts into it is one-sided. He may not, for instance, be able to express affection in his sexual relations, he may not have any affection in him to express. Or he may, like a drug addict, crave for a certain kind of sexual pleasure which looms so large in his mental horizon as to eclipse all other possibilities of sexuality. So he may turn his sexual partner into a means of satisfying his craving. His phantasy-life may be so absorbing that the people he takes into his sexual life are taken in as *dramatis personae* in an already scripted play; or it may be so repressed that he can find no excitement in sexual contact, his sensuality having become inaccessible to him with the repression of his phantasy-life. Thus whether sexuality takes the form of the obsessive pursuit of pleasure or of sexual intercourse with someone he is fond of though he can find no physical excitement in it, he will fail to find much sense in sexuality.

Freud knew that sexuality is something to which it is possible to give oneself. What one makes of it and whether or not it assumes a significance in one's life depends on that. However, the concepts in terms of which he discusses sexuality in the *Three Essays* do not permit Freud to explore this matter. The most that we find in this work is a hint that if sex is to make sense in a person's life it must be whole and not fragmented. This is not to exalt one form of sexuality and to condemn others. It is to show the possibilities of meaning or significance internal to different forms of sexuality. It is clear that Freud thinks that both sensuality and affection have a role to play in a sexual relationship that involves give and take, and that for this to be genuine these 'two currents' must be 'fused'. He further thinks that since 'the genital organisation' of a person's sensuality belongs to a more mature stage of his development it allows for the expression of less self-centred concerns. This is not to claim that genital sexuality is sufficient for a giving relationship, for it can certainly be selfish and tyrannical. But it is to claim that the other forms of sexuality belong with dependent modes of relationship where generosity is subordinated to need.

Someone may object that this is a misreading of Freud and that he expressed no preference for one form of sexual 'organisation' over another. He may further claim that for Freud conflict and suffering is the sole criterion of whether or not all is well with a person, and that this does not give him any basis for favouring one form of sexuality over another so long as the person himself has no reservations about it.

In his book *The Survival of English*, commenting on the trivialization of sex characteristic of our times, Ian Robinson sees such 'enlightenment' and hedonism ('the battle for happiness and the war against sexual boredom and frustration') as a symptom of the shallowness of our age. I said 'enlightenment': what is in question is the liberalization of sex, the high praise of uninhibited sexual activity, and the equation of sex with the pursuit of pleasure. He quotes a passage from Tolstoy's *The Kreutzer Sonata*:

> I fell because, in the set around me, what was really a fall was regarded by some as a most legitimate function good for one's health, and by others as a very natural and even innocent amusement for a young man. I did not understand that it was a fall, but simply indulged in that half-pleasure, half-need which, as was suggested to me, was natural at a certain age. I began to indulge in debauchery as I began to drink and to smoke. . .I remember that at once, on the spot before I left the room, I felt. . .so sad that I wanted to cry — to cry for the loss of my innocence.

He then quotes a critic's comment: 'In the sexual guilt that tormented Tolstoy we no longer perceive a problem. It has been taken care of by contraception.' His own comment is: 'Tolstoy's horror and terror are not the experience of sex I would wish for myself or for my friends, but they are reliable signs of the extreme significance he found in sex' (Robinson, 1975, p. 187). Robinson's point is that it is because sex mattered to Tolstoy, because he saw in it certain possibilities of relationship, that he lamented the way he was wasting it and felt guilty about cheapening such a precious gift.

Obviously to think of it as precious is to take a moral attitude towards sex; but one could not do so unless one saw the kind of significance it can have in human life. Robinson does not mention Freud, but others who are sensitive to the kind of issue he raises have sometimes blamed Freud's doctrines about sex and repression for the attitude towards sex which he criticizes. I do not believe that this blame is entirely justified. If anything that comes from Freud could be said to have influenced the development of this attitude it is the popular misrepresentation of his doctrines. Having said this, I will admit that there is something there which lends itself to such misrepresentation.

Freud was properly concerned to relieve certain kinds of misery and unhappiness. But this does not mean that his therapy aimed at removing obstacles to 'the pursuit of happiness', or that it was inspired by a philosophy that holds that we should aim at happiness in our lives. Freud did hold that repression is no way to solve one's problems and that in the end it can only add to one's misery. His therapy did aim at lifting repression even when this meant a temporary exacerbation of the patient's problems. The lifting of repression means the facing of what one fears or is ashamed of in oneself. But this is not the same thing as giving way to impulse — even if it increases the risk of doing so. Freud thought it was worth taking this risk, but he did not attach any value to acting on impulse or to indulging oneself. He never favoured taking the easy way; and the kind of therapy he developed did not offer easy solutions. On the contrary, it involves hard work and courage. The 'hedonism' which mars what he has to say at various points in his writings is little more than 'philosophical froth' and does not represent Freud at his most serious.

With regard to guilt about sex Freud never took the shallow

attitude which Robinson criticizes when he says that 'the removal of the possibility of guilt is the removal of the possibility of significance' (Robinson, 1975, p. 189). Freud knew that if there is guilt in a person about sex the reason for it is to be found in what sex means to him and, therefore, in what he puts into it and makes of it in his sexual activities and phantasies. The problem for the therapist is not to remove the guilt so that the patient can continue as before with an easy conscience; it is to enable him to change these activities so that what he does in them and what they mean to him no longer call for guilt. If the guilt he feels is genuine, the therapist will find in him the will to bring about such a change. It is true that some of Freud's philosophical pronouncements about morality obscure this by identifying morality with repression. On such a view guilt becomes little more than an irrational reluctance to indulge oneself based on a fear of punishment. However, Freud knew better than to think of guilt in this way.

In so far as the attention he gives to the perversions and auto-erotism dominates his discussion of sexuality in the *Three Essays*, Freud gives the impression of thinking that there is little more to sex than the pursuit of pleasure. But this is only one aspect of Freud's thought on sexuality. He also thought of it as a fundamental dimension of human relationship, a mode of affectivity in which human beings seek contact with each other.

I should like to make one final point about the passage from *The Kreutzer Sonata*. There is a difference between 'indulging oneself' and enjoying sex — taking delight in the other person in sexual intimacy. There is also a difference between 'experimenting with sex' and taking it seriously. If a young man or woman takes it seriously, does not indulge in it lightly, this does not mean that he or she is afraid of sex. Later on I shall refer to Malinowski's study of sex among the Trobriand islanders. He mentions there the institution of the *bukumatula* where adolescent boys and girls enter into sexual relations before marriage. From what I understand this involves some sexual promiscuity; but it would be a gross misunderstanding to describe what goes on there as either 'debauchery' or 'sexual experimentation'. Debauchery involves using the sexual partner, indulging oneself at his or her expense and without regard for him or her. It involves in addition looking down on her for cheapening herself in yielding to a relationship that lowers her. It always entails callousness and blindness to one's own heartlessness in treating someone in this way. One could go further and say that in not treating the other person as a human being and thus lowering him or her, one drags oneself down.

As for 'sexual experimentation' it is usually something artificial and self-conscious and involves the subordination of sex to a search for knowledge or pleasure. One will not learn much from sex, however, if one treats it in this way. As Simone Weil puts it in a letter to a former pupil: 'if you persist in your intention of experiencing all possible sensations — although as a transitory state of mind that is quite normal at your age — you will never attain to much.' She contrasts this with contact with what is real in life: 'The life which is truly real is not one that consists in experiencing sensations, but in activity. . .Those who live for sensations are parasites. . .compared with those who labour and create. . .I would add too that those who do not run after sensations are rewarded in the end by much that is more alive. . .than anything the sensation seekers experience.' She says: 'My conclusion. . .is not that one should shun love, but that one should not go out of one's way to try and find it, and especially so when you are very young' (Weil, 1951, pp. 34—5).

A biographer of Freud, Helen Walker Puner, mentions the following conversation between Freud and Jung during their visit to America in 1909 (Puner, 1959, p. 134):

Women, it seemed, were much on Freud's mind during his visit to America. With his stomach upset, he missed his wife's sympathetic ministrations. He joined Jung at breakfast in Worcester one morning only to remark bitterly: 'I haven't been able to sleep since I came to America. I continue to dream of prostitutes.' 'Well,' Jung shrugged, 'why don't you do something about it?' 'But,' Freud replied, appalled at the suggestion, 'I'm a married man'.

These words could mean something different in different people's mouths. They could be the expression of mere conventionality, or of a fear of sex — of sexual impulses that are held in check in the arrangement of marriage. Or they could be the expression of deep moral seriousness. There is no doubt what they signified in Freud's mouth: they came from a moral seriousness in him untouched by some of his views about the irrationality and illusory character of morality. As Drury puts it (1973, p. 127): 'It is clear from reading his biography and personal letters that the man Freud was more than his theory.'

I criticized Freud for obscuring the way in which a person enters into aspects of his sexuality as an individual. Freud does show some recognition of the fact that if sex is to make sense in a person's life it must be whole and not fragmented, but the morally neutral language in which he discusses sex in his *Three Essays* does not permit him to develop this thought. For the wholeness in question is bound up with the possibility of significance; and one can neither make sense of sex in one's life as an agent, nor compare what sex means to individuals in their different lives, as Freud attempts to do, without employing moral categories.

Freud's avoidance of moral language has more than one source. Among them we can single out philosophical presuppositions regarding the scientific nature of his enterprise in the *Three Essays* and his philosophical prejudices concerning morality. While I hope to comment on the latter there is one point I would like to make now. It was not simply as a result of philosophical prejudice that Freud avoided moral language in his practice as a psychotherapist. There are certain dangers in using moral language here and Freud was keenly aware of these. For a patient might take up a moral judgement not related to his own beliefs and use it for purposes of repression. Freud thought he had no business to intervene in a patient's life morally, to comment on the poverty of his sexual life, for instance, unless the patient himself felt impoverished by what his sexuality had come to be confined to. He wanted such a recognition to come from the patient himself. What he was not sufficiently alive to, however, was the opposite danger, namely that in avoiding moral language he might discourage patients from availing themselves of modes of expression to communicate genuine concerns. Where this is the case a patient can easily come to regard such a concern as unreal and lose touch with it.

I return, however, to Freud's emphasis on what are not so much components of 'adult sexuality' as of a sexuality in adults which has remained relatively fragmented. Freud knew that the tendencies at the core of these forms of 'fragmented' sexuality, for instance the tendency to look for pleasure in intercourse with a woman whose 'love' is for sale, are more common in the unconscious than we recognize. There, isolated and repressed, they impoverish a person's sexual life in two different and opposite ways. They do so when they are allowed into consciousness and indulged in. Endorsed, they prevent the agent from looking for and finding other possibilities of meaning in his sexual life. When, on the other hand, they remain repressed, the person's sexual life becomes an arrangement for avoiding the recognition of tendencies that stir up anxiety in him. Such a subordination of forms of adult sexuality to keeping at bay repressed tendencies drain them of any sense he could find there.

Repression and indulgence, as I said before, do not exhaust the field, and the former should not be confused with self-mastery. For when a person represses a desire or inclination he does not act on his own behalf but 'at the behest of the super-ego' (Freud, 1949d, p. 75). Besides, a desire he has repressed is not one that he has given up. Thus a person's moral beliefs play a very different role in repression from the one they play when he masters himself and resists a temptation or gives up a desire. He is differently related to them in the two cases. Similarly, to recognize in oneself what one finds intolerable is not to become morally insensitive to it. It is to face it as part of oneself without endorsing it. It is, therefore, not the same thing as giving oneself to it.

When a person turns from repression to indulgence his relation to the moral beliefs that were behind the repression remains unaltered, unless in time he loses those beliefs and, with them, the capacity to make sense of his sexuality. What Freud hoped for in psychotherapy was a change in the patient's relation to both his moral beliefs and his sexuality. Thus he said (1949b, p. 361) that a conflict between a repressive moral attitude and a repressed desire

is not resolved by helping one side to win a victory over the other.
It is true we see that in neurotics asceticism has gained the day;
the result of which is that the suppressed sexual impulses have
found a vent for themselves in the symptom. If we were to make
victory possible to the sexual side instead, the disregarded forces
repressing sexuality would have to idemnify themselves by symptoms. Neither of these measures will succeed in ending the inner
conflict, one side in either event will remain unsatisfied.

So the lifting of a repression was not regarded by Freud as an
end in itself. He believed it to be desirable because it provides
an opportunity for a person to renew his relation to both
sides of the conflict dividing him and to find himself in the
process — which finding involves coming to see possibilities
of sense excluded by remaining wedded to the tendencies
subjected to repression.

What in his theoretical writings on sex Freud represented
quasi-mechanically as the fusion of distinct components into
an amalgam is the same thing as what in his therapeutic work
he describes as the integration of the self. This, in turn, involves the transformation of what is integrated, be it moral
beliefs external to the will or desires and inclinations not
endorsed by the person: 'Where id or super-ego was, there ego
shall be' (Freud, 1933, p. 108). It is in this kind of transformation that a person finds new possibilities of sense in life.

Thus while Freud's theoretical treatment of sexuality is
open to serious objections, one must not forget that what he
says there is not divorced from what he knows in his therapeutic practice. While it is true that what is objectionable in
his theoretical writings on sex, as well as on morality, can
distort and vitiate that practice, it is equally true that the
insight which he shows in his practice can throw light on his
theoretical writings and reveal there perceptions overshadowed
by what is objectionable in the abstract formulations he gave
to his thoughts.

2

Oedipus Complex: The Child in the Family

1 The Oedipus Complex

Freud first formulated the idea of the Oedipus complex in connection with clinical observations and thought of it as a pathogenic phenomenon. As Malinowski points out (1955, pp. 153–4), originally the term 'complex' meant ' a pathogenous, repressed emotional attitude of the patient'. Thus a complex is something from which a person 'suffers'. Freud gave the Oedipus complex a prominent position in the aetiology of neuroses: 'The Oedipus complex is. . .the kernel of the neuroses' (1949b, p. 283). At least part of what he meant was that the conflict that a person still feels with regard to his parents lies at the basis of his later emotional and sexual difficulties in life. Those difficulties represent an enactment of this conflict in his current life, the repercussions of his doing so, and his reactions to them.

Freud later came to give the Oedipus complex a more general status. On his later view, it is not simply 'the kernel of the neuroses' but a fix into which each male child gets around the ages of four to six in the course of his emotional development. Some repress it, in which case it remains with them to haunt them for the rest of their lives and becomes the kernel of their later difficulties. Others are able to resolve the conflict and emerge from it with modified attitudes towards their parents and free from their dependency on them — although this 'resolution' and 'freedom' is a relative matter. The respective attitudes towards parents in the female child are reversed. On this later view the Oedipus complex, and the corresponding complex in women, are regarded as universal phenomena (Freud, 1949a, p. 104, fn. 2): 'Every new arrival on this planet is faced by the task of mastering the Oedipus complex; anyone who fails to do so falls a victim to neurosis.'

Freud came to attribute to it the power to explain the birth and development of culture itself. Hence his idea of totemism developing as a reaction to the Oedipus complex in much the way in which animal phobias do in individual children (see Freud, 1965). As Ernest Jones puts it (1949, pp. 83—4):

> In an important study of totemism. . .Freud has made it probable that this extensive institution is in a great part an elaborate defense against the Oedipus complex (incest and cannibalistic father-murder). Following hints put forward by Darwin and Atkinson, he has developed the view that this complex. . .played a vital part in the foundation of social and, ultimately, civilised life. Indeed, to the reactions of remorse and fear surrounding it he traces the beginnings of all law, morality and religion. So far-reaching has been the work that started in the treatment of hysterical pains!

Jones applies this idea in his explanation of such distinguishing features of a matrilineal society as those studied by Malinowski — the Trobrianders' avuncular family and their ignorance of the father's role in procreation: 'The motive in both cases is to deflect the hostility felt by the growing boy towards his father' (Jones, 1974, p. 159). The third part of Malinowski's book *Sex and Repression in Savage Society* is a detailed criticism of Jones's views. The move from an attempt to understand hysterical phobias to an explanation of social constellations and cultural phenomena, indeed of the very 'birth' of civilization, is both sweeping and riddled with confusion. Malinowski brings this out clearly and, in my view, disposes for good the conclusions of both Freud and Ernest Jones. But this is not a death-blow to Freud's idea of the Oedipus complex, and Malinowski does not think it is.

So what does the Oedipus complex amount to in Freud's

view? What is its significance? Freud sees it as one of the crises in an individual's life in his development towards independence and autonomy. We have already considered the infant's attachment to his mother and its character of dependence. This dependence is gradually modified as the infant grows into a young child. The first severance is forced on him with weaning. If this is traumatic it leaves a secret yearning in the child for his mother, a desire to recapture the exclusive relationship he had with her. But there are further stages of this severance, such as the arrival of a brother or sister, and going to school. The process continues with the developing ability of the child to look after himself, so that he is allowed to take over some of the functions carried out by his mother. This transition towards greater autonomy at each stage may be smooth or painful. If I speak of 'severance' I am thinking of the physical arrangements which foster emotional dependence. It is these that the growing child has to relinquish, not the link to his mother which is a link for life that cannot be rejected without emotional impoverishment.

So the exclusive character of the relationship with the mother cannot be maintained indefinitely. There are several reasons for this. The mother may not want it, and in any case other claims begin to impinge on her life — claims which until the time of weaning were to a certain extent kept in abeyance with the support of those others who also have some claim on the mother's attention. Secondly, the child himself develops interests and desires to venture forth, even when these are counterbalanced by his reluctance to let go of his mother's apron-strings. This reluctance may be strengthened by anything that increases the child's need for his mother, such as illness or pain. Among the claims that impinge on the mother's life and so stand in the way of an exclusive relationship with her are those made by the father. These are bound up with the special intimacy the father enjoys with the mother and his role in the family, including his role in the education of the child. He has to ensure that the child learns to curb some of his desires and may sometimes punish him in the process. Thus, while, on the whole, the mother is seen by the child as a source of indulgence, the father is seen as a source of authority. He stands in the way of indulgence, or is seen by the child as doing so. The child often manages to take steps towards greater independence by looking up to his father and treating him as a model to be emulated if he has a good relationship with him. Freud sees this relationship as based on 'identification'.

Freud did not suggest that the relationship between father and child cannot be co-operative. But he did suggest that progress towards greater independence involves some curbing, or transformation, of those impulses and desires in the child which he resists. In reality the father may not impose these changes on the child. He may manage to enlist the child's confidence and willingness, and he may have the mother's open support. Even then, at the level of phantasy, there will be some tendency in the child to divide these two movements in his own emotions, to side with the regressive one, seeing the movement towards greater independence as a wrench imposed on him by the father, and to resent it. This is what Freud calls the 'negative identification' with the father.

These different tendencies, according to Freud, exist side by side and in conflict with each other for a while. The conflict comes to a head around the ages of four to six, as the conflicting tendencies pick up new elements which reinforce them in the course of the child's growth. This conflict, when it comes to a head, constitutes the Oedipus complex. Freud attributes its coming to a climax to 'the irresistible advance towards a unification of mental life' (1949c, p. 61). This advance is the same as the one Melanie Klein sees as responsible, much earlier, for the infant moving from what she calls the 'schizoid position' to the 'depressive' one. Thus both Freud and Melanie Klein think that progress towards greater autonomy and deeper contact with reality demands greater toleration of pain.

Facing this conflict is painful for the child; staying with it, experiencing hatred and jealousy for his father, can be quite shattering. The fear of retaliation from his father is likely to throw him back on his mother for protection. The child may not be able to stay with this experience and live it through, and so he may 'repress' it. He may pretend he is not so attached to his mother, he may develop a submissive attitude towards his father, etc. If so, he will have lost his best chance to modify it, to grow out of it. These attitudes of defence will plague him in his future relationships and each time they don't work there or give rise to new conflicts the old wound will be reopened. The pain of the new conflicts will re-echo the pain he tried to bury as a child. If, however, in the course of his earlier dependency on his mother he had developed enough confidence in her to tolerate a greater distance from her, and if he has also enough good feelings for his father, he will be able to bear the experience without repressing the conflict. The mere fact that his worst fears are not realized, that his parents are able to take his bad temper and remonstrations without withdrawing their support, will give his anger the opportunity to spend itself out. It will also give him a chance to see his situation from a broader perspective so that it generates less emotional heat. This will enable the child to begin to take an interest in things outside his immediate family. In this way the Oedipus complex will be defused and the child will not continually be pulled back towards this original centre in later life.

2 Significance of the Oedipus Complex

I spoke of the Oedipus complex as one of the crises in an individual's life on the way to independence and autonomy. One may wonder why, if it is only one of these crises, Freud put so much emphasis on it — at the expense, it may seem, of later crises? There are, of course, many points of potential crisis in an individual's life, both before the formation of the Oedipus complex and subsequent to it. Different schools of psychotherapy have taken interest in different stages of emotional transition and the crises they may provoke. Otto Rank has spoken of a 'birth trauma'. Of course, the weaning of the child from the breast may develop into a crisis. Melanie Klein has taken great interest in the time in an infant's life when he is capable of experiencing guilt, grief and depression. She attached great significance to this for the later course of his life. This is closer to the Oedipus complex than any other developmental stage. Each is regarded by Melanie Klein and

Freud respectively as the period in which the foundations are laid for the individual's morality.

Then there are the potential crises relating to going to school and making new relations there, those relating to accepting authority without relinquishing newly-won independence. Because these problems are intertwined with the question of a reappraisal of where one stands with regard to one's parents, Erik Erikson talks of them as 'identity crises'. They concern the transition of an adolescent into adulthood, just as the Oedipus complex relates to the transition of a child into adolescence. Later there are the difficulties of making a marriage and becoming a father or mother. In each case the establishment of new bonds involves some relinquishment of the self which may, in turn, stir up older problems. Later still are difficulties connected with what to do with one's newly-won powers, how best to use one's talents, how to integrate one's deepest beliefs into their use so that one's life makes sense. Then later people may experience the difficulty of reconciling themselves to their waning powers and making way for others, and finally that of accepting death. Jung has shown an interest in some of these later difficulties and has argued that they call for a different sort of psychotherapeutic handling from the one advocated by Freud.

Let me add that these difficulties, which do not necessarily reach crisis proportions, may well overlap and often do so. They relate to growth and the taking on of new responsibilities, to developing the ability to stand on one's own feet and stick to what one believes, as well as to the relinquishment of one's selfishness, to making new relations and accepting old age. As such they are the lot of everyone and they are characteristic of different periods of an individual's life. Some relate to conditions of childhood, others to those of youth, and others still to those of middle and old age. There are, in addition, particular crises and difficulties not bound up specifically with any period of an individual's life, although they are part and parcel of the human condition — those that arise from the loss of loved ones and disappointments, those relating to illness and physical pain, and also crises of conscience and divided loyalties.

Some of Freud's critics, notably Jung, and also others such

as Viktor Frankl, have indicted Freud with a 'reductionism' that ignores this variety (Jung, 1966, pp. 66—7):

> We may distinguish a psychology of the morning of life and a psychology of its afternoon...The life of a young person is characterized by a general unfolding and a striving towards concrete ends....But the life of an older person is marked by a contraction of forces, by the affirmation of what has been achieved, and the curtailment of further growth.

Jung develops this in his paper 'The Stages of Life' in the same collection. Later on in the book he criticizes Freud for being 'one-sided' and for his neglect of the spiritual. He says that Freudian psycho-analysis is 'suited to people who believe that they have no spiritual needs or aspirations' (p. 259). 'Freudian analysis would brush all these matters [viz. religious and moral difficulties] aside as irrelevant. It holds the position that the basic problem is that of repressed sexuality, and that philosophical or religious doubts only mask the true state of affairs' (p. 268). 'The causes of a neurosis lie in the present as in the past' (p. 269).

It is perfectly true that in regarding the Oedipus complex as 'the peak of infantile sexuality' and 'the kernel of the neuroses' Freud did put a very large emphasis on sexuality and the past (i.e. on infantile sexuality) in his consideration of the roots of people's difficultties in their current life. It is true that he attributed the trouble that the Oedipus complex brings in later life to the individual's running away from it since the time of childhood. Jung's assessment that on Freud's view 'the basic problem is that of repressed sexuality' is, therefore, quite correct. It is also true that Freud thought that the foundation of a person's morality is laid down in his childhood (Freud, 1949d, pp. 47—8, 69): 'The super-ego is the heir of the Oedipus complex'. Further, he did not show adequate recognition of the positive character that morality assumes in people's lives when it is genuine; he thought of it too much as a repressive force. Thus when Frankl writes (1967, p. 154) that 'there are some authors who contend that...values are "nothing but defense mechanisms, reaction formations and sublimations" ', he is referring to a form of 'reductionism' encouraged by some things that Freud said. Such reductionism ignores the role of the spiritual in human life.

There is thus some justification for Jung's criticisms. However, I believe that the confusions which encouraged such reductionism are not endemic to Freud's thought and can be discarded without changing that thought in its essentials. Freud did not deny that the causes of a neurosis may lie in the present; he denied that they are confined to the present. In his response to the problems that face a man in his present situation he brings to it attitudes fixed in the past, not recognized by him. These complicate the problems and they rigidify his postures to them. Freud's view is that such a person would be freer to resolve these problems or, where they have no solution, to accept to live with them, if he could have greater awareness of the contribution made by his past. The reason why Freud puts so much stress on the Oedipus complex, on the conflicting attitudes of a person towards his parents, repressed in his childhood, is his belief that it contributes to, complicates and enhances the later difficulties. This does not mean that the later difficulties are simply echoes of the former ones, though they sometimes are; but that unless they are recognized and tackled directly they will stand in the way of the resolution of the more current ones.

In my estimation, if Freud is not too much concerned to give direct help to his patients in their current difficulties, this is not because he believes that these are 'nothing but' reflections of past difficulties. It is because he believes that once a patient has been helped over his earlier difficulties, those he has systematically avoided facing, he can be left on his own. Freud has faith that his patients are equipped to cope with these difficulties once the burden that cripples them has been removed. He does not see this as falling within the province of psychotherapy.

As for the difficulties that arise in earlier transitions in the development of a child or infant, Freud believed that these come to a head in the Oedipus complex. Melanie Klein, on the other hand, who carried out a more detailed investigation into early childhood and infancy, became convinced that there were transitions and difficulties here which needed singling out, just in the way that Freud had singled out the Oedipus complex for special attention. She believed that it was important to focus on them in analysis if lasting therapeutic help is to be achieved. I shall comment later on some aspects of her contribution (see chapter 5). I shall only say here that in my estimation she can be seen to be taking Freud's work forward and not deviating from it. I believe her contribution to be a major one and that some of her ideas redressed the one-sided treatment we find in Freud's work of the part a person's morality plays in his life.

3 Universality of the Oedipus Complex

When I said that there are other difficulties bound up with transitions in an individual's emotional development relating to conditions obtaining in relevant periods of his life, I spoke of these as 'the lot of everyone'. Certainly Freud regarded the Oedipus complex in this way. He thought that the conflicts that make up the Oedipus complex are an inevitable result of the stages in any individual's 'instinctual' development in early childhood. Yet this can be questioned and has been by Malinowski and other anthropologists. In my consideration of this question I shall confine myself to Malinowski. He combines an imaginative sympathy for Freud with intellectual integrity, and the questions he raises and discusses, especially in the third and fourth part of this book, *Sex and Repression in Savage Society*, are philosophical questions.

He shares with Freud a belief that what happens within the family lays the foundations of an individual's development. This is obviously at the heart of Freud's conception of the Oedipus complex. Further, Malinowski believes, and so does Freud, that the family is 'the cell of society', 'the starting point of all human organization', and that 'common sociability develops by extension of the family bonds and from no other sources' (1955, p. 165). In appreciation of Freud he makes the following two points that relate directly to Freud's idea of the Oedipus complex: (a) 'He was the first to state clearly that the family was the locus of sentiment formation.' (b) 'He also has shown that in the formation of sentiments the process

of elimination, of clearing away, is of paramount importance
and that in this process the mechanism of repression is the
source of conspicuous dangers' (p. 208).

In the first part of the book he raises the following question: 'Do the conflicts, passions and attachments within the
family vary with its constitution, or do they remain the same
throughout humanity?' (p. 19). This is in fact a philosophical
question about which he has a great deal to say in the second
half of the book. The first part of the book is descriptive and
comparative, and the question he investigates there is *how*
conflicts, passions and attachments within the family vary
with its structure and what the limits are to this variation. He
compares two types of family, known to him 'from personal
observation': 'the patrilineal family of modern civilisation, and
the matrilineal family of certain island communities in North-
Western Melanesia'. He says that they 'represent perhaps the
two most radically different types of family known to sociological observations' (p. 22). What is important to note from
our point of view is that in the matrilineal family the biological
father of the children, who is also the husband of the mother,
does not have the same role as the father in the patrilineal
family in Western society, and does not exercise the same
kind of authority on the children. In fact, the Trobrianders
are ignorant of the biological facts of procreation and do not
know the causal role the 'father', i.e. the mother's husband,
plays in the creation of the children. He generally plays with
the children and his relationship with them in their youth is a
purely friendly, tender one. The disciplining is carried out by
the 'uncle', the mother's brother. Descent identity and family
allegiance go through the mother's brother: 'Real kinship,
that is identity of substance, "same body", exists only through
the mother' (p. 23). The children are the heirs not of their
mother's husband, but of their mother's brother. The line of
descent is from uncle to nephew, and not from father to son,
and this determines who counts as kin and, therefore, with
whom sexual intimacy is to be avoided.

What this means is that the only candidate who could be
the centre of the kind of conflict Freud postulates is a man
who does not stand to the mother in the kind of relationship
which is presupposed in the idea of the Oedipus complex,

since this person is the mother's brother who 'can never be intimate with the mother, or therefore with her household': 'She recognises his authority, and bends before him as a commoner before a chief, but there can never be tender relations between them' (p. 24). The 'cannot' here refers to customs and traditions, backed by sanctions and taboos. On the other hand, the man who is intimate with the mother, her husband, is not the centre of such conflict. Malinowski examines in great detail the boy's changing relationship with both his mother and his 'father' or mother's husband, with special reference to its sexual aspect, in the different periods of his early life — infancy, babyhood, childhood and adolescence. He compares it carefully with the corresponding relationship, throughout these stages, in the patrilineal family in Western Europe, as seen in the bourgeoisie, the working classes, and in peasant communities. He finds some similarities and also striking differences, and he relates these differences to differences in the constitution of the two types of family, and the customs and traditions that enter into family relationships.

Let me briefly summarize his findings. In the first period of infancy the main difference relates to the role of the father who is more active in nursing the infant and playing with him. This 'gives him a far greater scope for forming ties of affection with his children' (p. 33). In the second period, babyhood, intimacy is allowed to develop between mother and child, as in our society. But the Melanesian mother is much more indulgent, for there is 'little training of the child' at this stage and 'hardly any moral education' (p. 35). Consequently there is little opportunity for severity, and the detrimental effects of its abuse are avoided. Weaning takes place much later than with babies in Western society, at a time when the child is already relatively independent: when he can run about eat practically everything, and follow other interests. Hence the first wrench is eliminated.

The father has a different status, behaves differently and is, therefore, seen differently. He is not the head of the family, he is not the main provider of food, and he does not transmit his lineage to his children. He has a different attitude to his wife, seldom quarrels with her, and he cannot exercise a permanent tyranny over her (p. 37). Though monogamy is strictly enforced, the husband does not take his wife for granted sexually or feel he has a right to her submission. In short he is no patriarch. The children don't see their mother as dependent on her husband, or feel his heavy hand on themselves. He is freer to give himself to his children in affection and to accept theirs in return (pp. 38—9).

Children are not subjected to any strict toilet training and Malinowski says that he has observed no infantile 'indecencies' or clandestine pastimes centring around excretory functions or exhibitionism (p. 43). They do not go through anything corresponding to Freud's period of anal erotic interests.

In the third period, childhood, from the age of five to puberty, 'the process of emancipation progresses gradually and constantly in an untrammelled, natural manner' (p. 46). The mother feels no jealous resentment or anxiety at the child's new-found independence. Malinowski relates this to the lack of educational interest of the mother in her children. Children form small juvenile communities, they roam about in bands and play on distant beaches. The games they play often take the form of sexual pastimes. They are thus initiated into the practices of sex by older companions. They cannot carry out the act properly but play at it, and so satisfy their curiosity and sensuality directly. The dominating interest in all this is genital. They imitate their elders. Natives allude to these as 'copulation amusements' and 'playing at marriage' and do not look upon it as reprehensible. They do not interfere or frown in disapproval. In these games the sensual pleasure is blended with some imaginative, romantic interest. The games do not take place in the house but otherwise the children are left entirely to themselves. The one restriction to this is the brother-sister taboo (pp. 57—8).

The father 'continues to befriend the children' and to 'teach them what they like and as much as they like'. But the children are less interested in him than they were before and prefer their small comrades. Still the father remains 'a helpful adviser, half playmate, half protector' (p. 48).

At this stage of the child's life 'the principle of tribal law and authority, the submission to constraint and to the prohibition of certain desirable things enters the life of a young girl or boy'. But it is represented not by the 'father' but by the maternal uncle. He is the head of the family and wields the *potestas*. But his influence is introduced into the child's life considerably later than that of the European father. Besides, he never enters into the intimacy of family life as the patriarchal father does. 'His power is exercised from a distance,' and it does not 'become oppressive in those small matters which are most irksome' (pp. 48—9). But it is the uncle who has the power, is idealized, and it is to him that the mother and children are subjected. It is he who introduces the child to duty, prohibition and constraint as well as to social ambition, traditional glory and pride in his lineage and kinship. Thus there is a sharp difference between the child's relation to his 'father' and his relation to his uncle. In the former co-operation is based on good will, in the latter it is largely based on custom and tribal law. There is also a sharp difference between the mother's relation to her husband and her relation to her brother, a difference which the child is aware of, and this makes a difference to his attitude towards them.

Malinowski points out that there are no initiation rites at puberty in the Trobriand islands and hence puberty 'does not constitute a sharp turning point as in those savage communities where initiation ceremonies exist' (p. 65). The boy gradually begins to take a more active part in economic pursuits and tribal occupations, and he also joins special houses, *bukumatula*, inhabited by groups of adolescent boys and girls, where he leads an active sexual life. The relationship with the mother contains little of the personal friendship, the mutual confidences and intimacy we find in the corresponding relationship in our society (p. 66). The 'father' suffers a temporary eclipse in the feelings of the adolescent, owing to the claims made on the latter's time, interests and emotions by the activities of the *bukumatula* and by the various duties towards the maternal uncle. But later friction with the uncle makes its appearance, the growing adolescent turns to his father and their friendship becomes settled for life (p. 67).

'The sister', as Malinowski put it, 'remains the only spot on the sexual horizon permenantly hidden.' She becomes 'indecent' as an 'object of thought, interest and feeling. . .Later on, as the personal experiences in sexuality develop, the veil of reserve separating the two thickens' (p. 69).

Malinowski's findings thus reveal a line of emotional development that differs from the one Freud sketched out in his *Three Essays*, and it does not culminate in the conflicting attitudes towards the parents, conscious and unconscious, which make up the Oedipus complex which Freud described as 'the peak of infantile sexuality'. Malinowski claims that what is in question is not simply a matter of the stages which instincts go through in their development. There is an aspect to the changes that take place, as well as to the resistances to them, which is the contribution of nature or instinct — for instance the physiological dependence of the infant on the mother which plays a large part in the infant's attachment to the mother, or the onset of puberty which introduces a new element into the adolescent's life. But the way a growing child learns to look at things and the kind of significance he finds in them, as he learns to speak and think; the forms of activity that go on around him and which what he learns enables him to enter into; what in turn he learns through his participation in these: all this introduces something completely new into his life. In short, one could call this the contribution of culture. It does not merely 'mould' the individual's life, as Malinowski often puts it, it *creates* many aspects of it (see chapter 6).

It is true, however, as both Freud and Malinowski appreciate, that the transitions which the child undergoes in his development to adulthood involve the relinquishment of positions of emotional dependence and the pursuit of pleasures which belong to them. The lure of new pastures which become available to the child through his physical, intellectual, moral and emotional development, give him a motive for relinquishing these old positions. The new pastures are provided by the forms of activity and interest characteristic of the culture within which the child grows up. In addition, there is the will to venture forth, to take up new interests, and the kind of adventurousness and initiative which appears in the course of the child's development, and varies from child to child. In the absence of complicating factors the child finds it easier to give up old positions if he is given the chance to live them out. It is true, however, that besides being lured by new pastures, the child is also often pushed into giving up positions which he is unwilling to relinquish. Freud has emphasized the father's role in this and has also pointed out that the child may resent this, and that often when he complies outwardly he continues to cling to the positions in question inwardly. What he clings to then goes on to characterize an aspect of the rest of his life.

Malinowski's research reveals that among the Trobrianders 'the detachment from the mother, carried out. . .at every stage more easily and more thoroughly than with us, with fewer premature and violent suppressions, is achieved in a more complete and harmonious manner' (pp. 66–71). There is, consequently, no residue of the early attachment to the mother in the unconscious which is one of the components of the Oedipus complex. In addition, within the structure of the family, the father does not enter into the kind of relationship with the boy or his mother to make him the object of the kind of feelings which develop in the Oedipus complex. The fact of his sexual intercourse with the mother may be a necessary condition for the development of an Oedipus complex, but it is by no means sufficient. What more is needed, absent in the Melanesian social set-up, is that he should have certain rights over the mother and children, and wield some power within the family and in the education of the children. For the child to develop feelings of hatred, resentment and jealousy towards him, he must think of his father as pushing him aside, as ruling over him, and he must represent his father as an ideal which he cannot reach. In the following section I shall consider the question of whether he can do so in phantasy when there is no basis in reality for his seeing his father in this light.

Malinowski's conclusion is that it is the patriarchal society and the structure of the family within it that provide the conditions for the development of the Freudian Oedipus complex. Where the conditions are absent we do not find the Oedipus complex. Accepting many of Freud's ideas in the first part of his book, Malinowski speaks of a 'family nuclear complex' which takes different forms in different societies.

In our society it takes the form of the Oedipus complex. In the matrilineal Melanesian society it takes a different form which Ernest Jones christens the 'avuncular complex'. The components of the Oedipus complex are hate for the father, largely unconscious, and repressed desire for the mother. Whereas 'in the matrilineal society. . .though the child has developed very definite sentiments towards its father and mother, nothing suppressed, nothing negative, no frustrated desire forms a part of them' (1955, p. 72). The reasons he gives are: (a) the tolerant attitude towards infantile sexuality; (b) the fact that the child's sensuous clinging to his mother is allowed to take its natural course until it plays itself out and is 'diverted' to other bodily interests;[1] (c) the father's very different role in the family.

Malinowski sees the 'family complex' in Melanesian society as centring around the maternal uncle and the sister. While I do not doubt that the uncle and the sister may well be the centre of the kinds of sentiment Malinowski describes in his book, I doubt that at least the sister and the uncle's relation to her would constitute sufficiently strong magnetic centres of unconscious phantasy to justify the use of the term 'complex' here. Surely the important point is that Malinowski's detailed study of a concrete example brings out how much more complicated are the conditions for the formation of an Oedipus complex than Freud imagined. As he puts it, psychoanalysis provides only 'a partial explanation' of the formation of the Oedipus complex (1955, p. 76). It is not a universal phenomenon, as Freud imagined; its existence presupposes that certain social conditions obtain.

Of course there may be other criticisms to be made of what Freud claimed in this connection or of some of the presuppositions implicit in it. But so far, although I believe Malinowski's conclusions to be extremely important, I do not see that acceptance of them detracts from Freud's contribution to psychology. What it detracts from and, in fact, completely destroys is Freud's use of the concept of the Oedipus complex in explanations of cultural phenomena and of the birth of civilization in *Totem and Taboo*. For if the existence

---

[1] I have put 'diverted' in inverted commas because of the presupposition of identity it brings into this diagnosis, one which needs justification.

of the Oedipus complex presupposes the reality of certain social conditions, it cannot be used to explain the emergence of culture and civilization. This is what Malinowski argues successfully against Freud and Ernest Jones in the third part of his book.

His debate is with Ernest Jones who, in 'Mother-right and the Sexual Ignorance of Savages' (Jones, 1974), took up Freud's defence against the background of Malinowksi's findings described in the first two parts of his book. Malinowski had argued that in the matrilineal society of the Trobriand islanders the conditions necessary for the formation of an Oedipus complex are absent and that, as a matter of fact, no such complex was revealed to observation. Ernest Jones argues that those conditions themselves, especially mother-right and the ignorance of paternity, must have evolved as a *defense* against the recognition of the Oedipus complex and are, therefore, in that sense evidence for its existence: 'To us the conception of a family where the father plays such a subordinate part, being to a great extent replaced by an uncle, certainly seems strange and needful of explanation' (Jones, 1974, p. 151). 'The motive. . .in both cases [viz. ignorance about paternal procreation and the institution of mother-right] is to *deflect the hostility felt by the growing boy towards his father*' (p. 159). Jones's use of the term 'motive' is significant here and goes together with his analysis of the development of social institutions and phenomena along the same lines as psycho-analysis treats individual development and symptom-formation.[2] He inherits this from Freud and I shall comment on it in chapter six.

Malinowski brings out well the metaphysical character of Jones's arguments. To claim that mother-right and ignorance of paternity are defenses against the recognition of the Oedipus complex one has to have independent evidence for the existence of the Oedipus complex (Malinowski, 1955, pp. 129—30):

> If, however, as Dr. Jones seems fully to admit, the attitudes typical of the Oedipus complex cannot be found either in the conscious or unconscious; if. . .there are no traces of it either in

[2] Thus see his comments on the myth of the Virgin Mary in Jones, 1974, pp. 161—2.

Trobriand folk-lore or in dreams and visions, or in any other
symptoms. . .where is then the repressed Oedipus complex to be
found?

What Malinowski rejects is the concept of the Oedipus
complex as 'something absolute', 'the primordial source. . .of
everything' (pp. 128–9), as something 'genetically transcendent' (p. 131). 'Dr. Jones. . .regards the complex as the *cause*,
and the whole sociological structure as the *effect*' (p. 126).
Thus conceived the existence of the Oedipus complex is an
a priori assumption and as such 'metaphysical' in the pejor-
ative sense of the term. Malinowski's own view is that 'the
nuclear family complex is a functional formation dependent
upon the structure and upon the culture of a society. It is
necessarily determined by the manner in which sexual restrictions are moulded in a community and by the manner in
which authority is appointed' (p. 129). This is a great step
forward, but it seems to me that it suffers from a reversal of
the 'individualism' I attributed to Freud's and Jones's thought.
I suggested that Jones's use of the term 'motive' in connection
with the explanation of social phenomena was part of this
individualism. Similarly Malinowski's use here of the term
'functional formation' is part of his inclination to treat the
Oedipus complex almost as if it were a social institution. He
speaks of the two components of the Oedipus complex, the
tendency to incest and the revolt against authority, as the
'two main perils of humanity', each created and curbed by
culture (p. 195). He argues that 'between the human parent
and child under conditions of culture there *must* arise incestuous temptations' and that 'these temptations have to be met
and. . .repressed in mankind, since incest and organised family
life are incompatible' (p. 164, [my italics].)

We must note that the aim of achieving or maintaining
'organized family life', for the sake of which Malinowski
claims repression is carried out, does not belong to the individual. Thus the formation of the Oedipus complex is given a
social explanation. Yet there is a difference between claiming
that certain social conditions underlie the possibility of the
formation of the Oedipus complex so that in their absence it
would be idle to expect to find it, and representing it as the
product of certain social conditions owing to certain tenden-

cies endemic to culture. This stronger claim which Malinowski makes raises questions just as much as the stronger claim concerning the Oedipus complex in Freud's writings on culture and civilization.

Malinowski's criticism of this stronger claim made by Freud in *Totem and Taboo* is devastating: 'The theory of Freud and Jones tries to explain the origins of culture by a process which implies the previous existence of culture and hence involves a circular argument' (p. 137). His critical argument is set out concisely in the chapter entitled 'The Primordial Cause of Culture'.

4 Some Other Criticisms

Someone may argue that the absence of conditions that would be conducive to the formation of an Oedipus complex is no reason why it should not flourish all the same, since unconscious attitudes are triggered off as much by phantasy as by reality. Thus in his *New Introductory Lectures* when discussing the genesis of the super-ego, which he describes as 'the heir of the Oedipus complex', Freud points out what he calls a 'contradiction', namely that while the super-ego is formed by the 'introjection' of parental authority, its strictness does not correspond to the strictness of parental authority. Sometimes its strictness seems to be inversely proportional to the strictness of the parents (Freud, 1933, p. 90):

> If the parents have really ruled with a rod of iron, we can easily understand the child developing a severe super-ego, but, contrary to our expectations, experience shows that the super-ego may reflect the same relentless harshness even when the up-bringing has been gentle and kind, and avoided threats and punishment as far as possible.

Freud's explanation is that this harshness originates from the child's hostility towards his father. The child projects this hostility onto his father and so the parental authority he introjects bears the burden of his own projection. Could it not be argued, similarly, that even when the father has no rights over the mother, exercises no authority on the children, and does not determine lineage, the mere fact that he is the mother's constant sexual partner is sufficient to constitute a kernel around which the child can weave phantasies that breed jealousy and hostility?

There are two answers to this question. The first is an empirical one provided by Malinowski, namely that no traces of such feelings are to be found in any of the likely places where Freud has looked for expressions of the unconscious. The second answer, which supplements Malinowski's arguments, rules out the possibility of the Oedipus complex here. It is true that phantasy does not need the backing of reality to get going. We know well enough that disturbed children come not only from homes where they were neglected and badly treated but also from 'good' homes. But while phantasy does not need the backing of reality, it makes use of and therefore presupposes some contact with forms of understanding and feeling which are themselves rooted in the life of the society to which the child belongs. It cannot, therefore, be entirely independent of features of this life. The differences which Malinowski depicts are relevant to whether or not it is conceivable that the Trobriand child will develop those attitudes towards his parents that constitute the Oedipus complex.

Let us agree then that the possibility of the Oedipus complex presupposes the existence of certain conditions. Does it follow that where these conditions obtain the Oedipus complex must develop? The affirmative answer claims that the Oedipus complex is universal within the patriarchal family. Malinowski seems to support this view and, by implication, so does Freud.[3] On this question Malinowski seems to treat individuals primarily as members of a particular society with a distinctive culture. But from claims made at this level nothing specific follows about particular individuals. So are we to go even further than Malinowski and abandon the view that the Oedipus complex is at least universal within the patriarchal family?

Some psycho-analysts, notably Karen Horney in the United States, have taken this line. Horney believes that the kind of unconscious attitudes contained in the Freudian Oedipus

---

[3] Although, as we have seen, Freud holds the stronger view that the universality of the Oedipus complex transcends cultural boundaries.

complex arise only when *special* conditions obtain in the family — not conditions pertaining to the structure of the family, as in Malinowski's view, but conditions created by the individual behaviour of its members, members of the patriarchal family. These fall under two headings: those that prematurely draw out the child's sexuality and increase his dependence, and those which through neglect or hostile treatment increase his anxiety. We have seen that to imagine that phantasies which presuppose a patriarchal social setting can develop in an altogether different social setting is a symptom of confusion. On the other hand, to think that for such phantasies to develop one needs not only the relevant social setting but positive provocation is to swing to the opposite extreme and to underemphasize the contribution of unconscious phantasy. In this respect I would put Karen Horney on the opposite side relative to Melanie Klein.

Horney does not allow the idea of the Oedipus complex as a stage in the individual's development in the patriarchal family, a stage with its own special emotional problems for the child. For Freud the problems themselves are not neurotic, but the individual child's 'solutions' may be. They are so when they involve repression. Neurotic solutions create further problems and the individual's response to these create still further problems. Karen Horney shows a lively recognition of this. But she does not sufficiently recognize that there are problems endemic to emotional development in human beings irrespective of the society in which they are brought up, although what the problems are vary with the culture of the society in question. Freud overlooked this variation, but he recognized the fundamental character of the problems, as does Malinowski. Horney, on the other hand, recognizes the variation but loses sight of the problematic character of individual development irrespective of its social context.

Freud's contribution in formulating the idea of the Oedipus complex, in my estimation, lies here. He recognized that there are emotional problems bound up with the development of the child, problems concerning his relationships with his parents. These centre around his attachments and emotional dependence, how much restriction he can take from his parents and how much he can give up for them without resentment. At the core of these problems is the conflict between his dependent attachment to his mother, the ideal of greater independence embodied in his father, and the threat of turning this in phantasy into a tyrannical assertion of paternal rights over the mother, reacting to it on that basis. Freud's contribution lies in his depiction of the sexual character of the child's attachment to his mother, of the ambivalence that characterizes his relationship with his father, of the way the child deals with the problems these raise for him, the use he makes of 'projection', 'introjection' and 'identification' in response to these problems, and the way in which the particular character of his response to them influences the course of his later development and life. One of the big distinctions Freud makes here is that between gradual sensual detachment from the mother and consolidation of affectionate feelings towards her on the one hand, and apparent detachment with an underlying emotional clinging to her on the other. Another is that between the ability to obey without loss of autonomy and conscious submission impregnated with unconscious resentment. Both distinctions enter into Freud's conception of the resolution or dissolution of the Oedipus complex. Where the Oedipus complex is repressed it leaves behind emotional dependence or anxiety in accepting intimacy, placatory submissiveness or a rebellious inability to submit to authority. There is no aspect of life that may not be affected by these problems and attitudes.

Freud believes that a stable relationship with the parents presupposes love and affection, and that the capacity for such love can only be achieved when conflicting emotions do not hinder autonomy and do not, in turn, reinforce dependency. They will do so until they are faced and lived through. This is what lies at the basis of Freud's idea of the dissolution of the Oedipus complex. What is in question is not, as Karen Horney has it, the solution of problems which face some individuals in their childhood and not others. As Malinowski puts it perceptively: 'Freud. . .was the first to state that the family was the locus of sentiment formation' (1955, p. 208). This is what lies at the centre of the stress Freud put on the Oedipus complex when he described it as 'the peak of infantile sexuality' and 'the kernel of the neuroses'.

3

Love and Sexuality

1 Sexual Love

In the last two chapters we have examined Freud's views about the nature of human sexuality and his claim that it exists in the life of the child, albeit in a different form from the one it takes after puberty. Freud's view is that it can exist in the life of the young child independently of love or, indeed, of any relationship, viz. 'auto-erotism'. But it also enters the child's love for his parents, in which case his love is the expression of sex and, as such, is sexual in character.

Indeed, the child's love for those who care for him can be seen as the expression of the child's sexuality, as Freud does. But equally his sexuality, or some of it, can be seen as the expression of his love. This is how Melanie Klein and her followers look at it. One could say that love and sexuality are different aspects of the same phenomenon here, like the Jastrow figure of the duck-rabbit. But which aspect one brings into prominence is obviously important for the way one goes on to think about the child's relationship to his parents and the way this influences his development and later relationships.

Having seen the child's love as a phenomen of his sexuality, Freud went on to think of all love as essentially sexual in character. This needs criticism. The infant's and young child's life is very largely confined to his body and revolves around his bodily functions and reactions. This body constitutes almost his sole medium of contact with his mother. She cares for him by attending to it and he responds to that care through bodily reactions. Thus the infant's response to the mother who feeds him at the breast may be one of pleasure in or gladness for what she gives him. It is this sensual love, finding expression in the infant's response, that is claimed to be 'sexual'. Such characterization is meant to emphasize its affinities to adult sexuality without denying its differences from it.

D. H. Lawrence, to give one example, rejects this characterization because of his interest in the unique character of adult sexuality and so emphasizes the differences (1977, p. 102):

> Sex. . .is present from the moment of birth, and in every act or deed of every child. But sex in the real sense of dynamic sexual relationship, this does not exist in a child, and cannot exist until puberty and after. True, children have a sort of sex consciousness. Little boys and little girls may even commit indecencies together. And still it is nothing vital. It is a sort of shadow activity. . .It has no profound effect.

Lawrence means that it does not, in the child's life, have the possibilities that belong to sexual passion in adult life. If a follower of Freud were to insist that it does have a 'profound effect', he and Lawrence would be speaking at cross purposes.

In any case the possibilities that belong to sexual passion in adult life come from that life. The point that I wish to make now is that if in the very young child's life love is inevitably an expression of his sexuality this has to do with the limits of that life and the way these are determined by his body. As he grows up and his life changes, as he acquires language and, therefore, thought, the world in which he lives changes, he comes to have new horizons. Love in this new world need no longer be something that is confined to sex; and sex itself can assume a new significance there, as Lawrence shows in some of his novels.

From the fact that love and sex can be the same thing not only in infantile life but also especially in adult life one should not draw any general conclusions concerning the sexual character of love. Freud did do so. He thought of love as necessarily an expression of sex. It is interesting to note that he uses two different words in this connection: 'libido' and 'eros'. When he speaks of eros he is thinking of the attributes which sex acquires through its identification with love — such attributes as creativity. Hence the way he contrasts it with a 'death instinct', the main expression of which is destructiveness. Thus while his identification of love with sex sometimes limits his understanding of what love can bring to a person's life, at other times it is just this which he means to bring into prominence. But more of this later. At the moment I am concerned with the limitation in his understanding of love — sexual love included.

In *Group Psychology and the Analysis of the Ego* Freud tells us that we call many different things 'love' and that among these things the love between man and woman, 'sexual love', occupies a central position. They differ in accordance with the person's conscious desires and aspirations with regard to what he loves, although each exhibits various degrees of affinity to sexual love (see Freud, 1949c, pp. 37—8). But is it these manifest affinities that give them their sexual character, or is it some hidden ingredient which they share with sexual love? Freud is inclined to think the latter: 'All these tendencies are an expression of the same instinctive activities.' This is an instance of the 'essentialism' from which he is on the whole free in his *Three Essays*. He writes further down that 'even in its caprices the usage of language remains true to some kind of reality' (p. 71). It is capricious in that 'it gives the name "love" to a great many kinds of emotional relationship'. But the application of the name is not really capricious or arbitrary, as it may appear, for it is responsible to 'some kind of reality'. So far this is not necessarily a form of essentialism; whether or not it is so would depend on Freud's view as to the nature of this reality. It would depend on whether he regards the manifest affinities sufficient to justify the use of the word in the diverse cases he mentions, or requires something further, a reality underlying these affinities (see Dilman, 1978). There is evidence that he does make such a requirement. His view that all love is essentially sexual in character goes with that.

Thus Freud suggests that the differences are more apparent than real, that as far as the 'lover's' unconscious attitudes and desires are concerned what we find in these diverse cases is more or less the same: 'A psychology which will not or cannot penetrate the depths of what is repressed regards tender

emotional ties as being invariably the expression of tendencies
which have no sexual aim, even though they are derived from
tendencies which have such an aim' (Freud, 1949c, p. 118).
By way of substantiation Freud cites two kinds of case. In
the first kind, in the course of a purely tender relationship, or
one based on esteem and admiration, sexual desires make
their appearance: 'It is well known how easily erotic wishes
develop out of emotional relations of a friendly character,
based upon appreciation and admiration, between a master
and a pupil, between a performer and a delighted listener'
(p. 119). He mentions 'how easily even an intense religious
tie can revert to ardent sexual excitement' (p. 119). But these
cases prove nothing about the character of love, friendhsip,
appreciation and admiration. They only show that in *some*
cases, for example, a religious tie masks or is the vehicle of
sexual feelings, and in others it is transformed and becomes
sexualized.

In the second kind of case, two people are brought together
by sexual attraction and then, in time, affection grows and
cements their relation. Freud speaks here of the sexual
tendencies being 'transformed into' a lasting and purely tender
tie (p. 119). What is true is that in these cases affection grows
within a relationship that is based on sensuality and transforms
the character of the sex in the relationship. For with the
development of affection the whole affective orientation of
the couple towards each other changes and with this what
part of themselves they give to each other and so what sex
comes to mean to them. It is true that we can distinguish
between the sensual and the tender aspects of the relationship; but this does not mean that they are two separate things
joined together. We can say here that these two people's
sensuality has become a form or an expression of their affection, and also that their affection is a form which their sensual
longing for each other has come to take. This is what Freud
must mean by the sensual and affectionate currents coming
to be 'fused'. But the change in each is more like what happens in a chemical reaction. You can identify the elements
that have entered into the fusion, but you cannot say that
they have the same character now as before. Thus from the
sexual character of the affection in these cases one is not

justified in concluding that of necessity affection is a state of sexuality. It is *one* of the states of sexuality, which means that it *can* have a sexual character and that a sexual relationship is one of its homes. But it has other homes and other faces.

This is just as true of love. We call many different things 'love', we speak of 'loving' many different things, and we use the word 'love' in different ways in these different connections — 'I love you,' and 'I'd love to have a holiday in the Bahamas.' Thus a man can love a woman, or a woman can love a man. We often distinguish this by speaking of 'sexual love'. Where a man loves a man we speak of 'homosexual love' and where a woman loves a woman we speak of 'lesbian love'. Then we speak of parental love, of maternal, paternal and filial love. Again a person may care for and love an animal he keeps as a pet. We often speak of other things that a person cares for and looks after as things that he loves —his garden for instance. We speak of friendship as involving love, of love of one's country or 'patriotism', of 'love of one's neighbour' in the religious sense, and of 'the love of God'. We speak of something one enjoys and appreciates as something one loves — a piece of music, a work of art, or the work in which one is engaged. And we also speak of the way one puts oneself out, holds oneself together, and works in caring for something or making it grow as 'a labour of love'. Thus creation is described as a labour of love.

This already takes in a wide area of human endeavour, relationship and affectivity, and covers a great variety of phenomena in which human personality finds expression. The desires and attitudes that belong to love in these different cases, and the qualities of character that flourish as aspects of the love exemplified in them, vary a great deal from case to case. Thus we may speak of affection or fondness, or friendship, loyalty, concern, admiration, appreciation, sympathy and compassion as forms of love. Though they differ from each other — admiration and compassion for instance — they are expressions of tendencies, impulses and orientations which constitute the many faces of love.

There are many such tendencies and impulses, and none of them are necessary to love. Any one or more of them may be in the background or altogether absent; or they may dominate the 'lover's' actions and affectivity, they may be exaggerated and even warped. Thus in sexual love the desire for contact and communion with the beloved may eclipse the concern for his or her welfare and take on the form of possessiveness out of which may grow jealousy. We may say that in such a case jealousy is an expression of love, of a possessive love, a love which craves to keep the relationship with the beloved completely exclusive. We can easily understand this craving as part of sexual love, and we know that where the lover makes no claim at all to some form of exclusiveness, he has become indifferent to the beloved and stopped loving her. For wanting the other person is part of what we understand by sexual love, and wanting in the sphere of sex does not tolerate sharing when it is passionate. On the other hand, devoid of all regard for the beloved and shorn of the bond of affection it becomes an expression of lust. As Freud points out, it is affection that gives permanence to a sexual relationship. But his understanding of the way affection contributes to such permanence is inadequate: 'Those sexual instincts which are inhibited in their aims have a great functional advantage over those which are uninhibited. Since they are not capable of really complete satisfaction, they are especially adapted to create permanent ties' (pp. 118–19).

The point, however, is not that affection cannot be completely satisfied so that the person in question stays around for further satisfaction. This is a grotesque misrepresentation of the permanence of which human relationships are capable. The point rather is that affection does not seek satisfaction but is orientated towards the individuality of the other person. Thus in a paper called 'Desire and Affection', J. L. Stocks contrasts it with desire (1969, pp. 38–43):

> For desire what is significant is the general character which enables a given individual to provide the appropriate satisfaction, the eatability of a roll of bread, the drinkability of a glass of wine. The object of desire is the mere vehicle of a motion which ends in the organism in which it begins. This means that any individual object offered for use in the satisfaction of desire may be replaced without loss or disturbance by some other individual object possessing the same general character. . . .

> But of course desire is not the whole of life. In man's mind. . .
> there is another principle at work. . .This principle I will call
> affection. . .It is to be seen at work. . .in any act or activity for
> which a particular thing or person has its own peculiar significance
> and is irreplaceable by another particular of the same kind. . .The
> principle of affection creates relations of individuals in respect of
> their individuality.

I said that wanting in sex devoid of affection and of regard
for the person wanted becomes lust. I did not mean to equate
this wanting in sex with desire in the sense in which Stocks
speaks of it — what one may call 'generalized desire'. By lust
I meant the wanting in sex not sustained by affection, not
transformed by regard. This wanting is passion, not pure
desire; it is directed to a particular person, not towards pleasure.

I did not, secondly, mean to suggest that affection is the
only form of bond or affectivity in sexual love in which the
other person counts as a person. Affection for another person
can be very deep, but it is a calm form of affectivity. Whereas
in sexual love as a passion the beloved excites the lover. What
excites him are the beloved's attributes seen by him under
the aspect of beauty. Here the lover is not fond of the beloved,
he is held spell-bound by her. She is a magnetic centre to
him. This is not simply a question of desire, although sexual
desire comes into it. But its satisfaction merely adds to the
fascination he finds in the beloved; it reveals further facets of
her personality that increase the wonder he feels for her.
Unless, that is, his love is an illusion and the reality of its
object disappoints or disillusions him. It is in this that sexual
love differs from lust. Lust is inspired by the desirability of
the beloved, love by her beauty. That is why love has the
possibility of depth; lust does not.

We are talking about *one* form of love which is a phenomenon of sex, and I have said that it can in no way be reduced
to desire. At the core of it is the magnetism of beauty. This,
in turn, cannot be understood in terms of the idealization of
qualities which one finds desirable — as Freud is inclined to
do. Hence love as a sexual passion is a phenomenon of civilization. For a person must find something beautiful if he is to
be moved by its beauty. This vision, and such reactions as

wonder and humility which belong to it, presupposes thoughts
and attitudes that bring in a whole culture with its literature
and art, its poems and songs of praise, its forms of worship
and thanksgiving. Beauty is something we praise, something
we like to contemplate, and we find that it is always more
than what we can say about it. Hence we often speak of
beauty as 'mysterious'. We find that nothing that we can do
can quite match up to what it inspires in us. Sexual love
which is inspired by beauty partakes of this character.

I used to think that Proust's description of the inaccessibil-
ity of Albertine is an expression of Marcel's inability to make
contact with things, 'to break out into the world', of his
'sensation' of being 'always enveloped in, surrounded by our
own soul'. It certainly is that; but not simply that. It is also
an expression of the way in which what we find beautiful
holds us by the fact that we cannot touch it (Proust, 1952,
Pt. II, vol. x, pp. 248–9):

> At moments, in Albertine's eyes, in the sudden flush of her cheeks,
> I felt as it were a gust of warmth pass furtively into regions more
> inaccessible to me than the sky, in which Albertine's memories
> unknown to me, lived and moved. Then this beauty which, when
> I thought of the various years in which I had known Albertine
> whether upon the beach at Balbec or in Paris, I found that I
> had but recently discovered in her, and which consisted in the
> fact that my mistress was developing upon so many planes and
> embodied so many past days, this beauty became almost heart-
> rending. Then beneath that blushing face I felt yawned like a gulf
> the inexhaustible expanse of the evenings when I had not known
> Albertine. I might, if I chose, take Albertine upon my knee, take
> her head in my hands; I might caress her, pass my hands slowly
> over her, but, just as if I had been handling a stone which encloses
> the salt of immemorial oceans or the light of a star, I felt that I
> was touching no more than the sealed envelope of a person who
> inwardly reached to infinity.

In what way is the sudden flush of Albertine's cheeks part
of the heartrending beauty in her before which Marcel feels
helpless? It is such when in Marcel's apprehension it is connected with the memory of days he spent with her and her
friends in Balbec, beside the sea, described in an earlier volume
(*A l'ombre des jeunes filles en fleurs/Within a Budding Grove*).

These are memories of days not only when he had known her but also when her life, mingled with that of the group of young girls with whom he played but to which he was an outsider, offered rich pastures for his imagination. The fact of her having a life necessarily separate from and independent of Marcel's became for him an endless subject of imagination. The terms in which Marcel imagines that life fill him with both longing and wonder, exaltation and jealousy. But the main point to which I want to come is that these terms belong to a language, literature and mode of sensibility which exist independently of Marcel and to which Proust has made a major contribution, although they are at the same time the terms most suited to Marcel Proust's individual psychology. Without them he could neither remember 'so many past days', think of what life would be without her, nor imagine 'the inexhaustible expanse of the evenings' when he had not known Albertine. And without the support of such memory and imagination all the fullness and magic she has for him would dwindle into nothing.

To see a person in his or her fullness, that is as a person with thoughts, feelings and intentions, with a past about which he may have regrets and a future in connection with which he has hopes and anxieties, some of which one knows, others about which one may be curious or apprehensive, all this presupposes the kind of life we live with language, the kind of life which makes it possible for one to think, imagine, take an interest in and show concern for others. Such a life is just as necessary for the other person to have the fullness and humanity of a person. I have discussed this question elsewhere[1] and it is not my intention to elaborate on it now. To see a person in his or her magic, to respond to that magic, to be captivated by it, this has often been attributed to 'the chemistry of the sexes'. While this is not wrong, it fails to mention everything which the workings of that chemistry presupposes.

What would show the existence of such magic in a relationship between lovers? What would show that they are captivated by each other's magic? What would show that their

---

[1] See Dilman, 1975, Pt. II, especially chapter 2.

desire for each other is lit up by it and is not just straight-forward, ordinary sexual desire? The answer is, surely, the terms in which they think of each other, the significance which each has in the other's life, the way they miss each other, the character of their longing, the despair with which the possibility of a life without the other would fill the soul of each. These terms and this mode of sensibility come from what Rush Rhees has called 'the language of love' (1969, pp. 122–3). And where has this language developed primarily but in literature, in love poetry and songs, novels and drama?

The lover finds his individuality in a life which has produced such literature and can boast of a literary heritage that stretches back into the past. His own life bathes in it, even if he is himself not acquainted with most of this literature. Its forms of sensibility and modes of expression are available to him through the life he shares with others — if not pure then in their adulterated varieties. They are in any case part of the language he speaks. The dependence between what happens in the lives of individual people and the literature which belongs to the language they speak is two-way: the literature portrays incidents in those lives and shows us what men are capable of, it shows us what love is like for different people and in different circumstances, the different forms it can take, its power for good and evil, its glory as well as its power to destroy. But it also constitutes aspects of the character of those lives, contributes to the determination of what men are capable of envisaging and experiencing, through the modes of expression it develops in the language they speak.

Earlier I mentioned the fact that beauty is something that we wonder at and praise. Without these responses what would the recognition of beauty be among men? It would be noth-ing, there would be nothing corresponding to such recognition. We could not say that beauty played a role in the lives of men. The contemplation of beauty is a further extension of these responses and reactions. We could speak of such reac-tions as 'natural' to men in the sense that we find them wherever men have formed communities and developed a life they share — I mean such responses as praise, awe, gratitude, dedication. But though natural they could not have existed without the language in which they are given expression. The development of these responses among men *is* the development of the language of praise and worship, the terms in which men express the value of what they praise, exalt it and reflect on it. This language, through the responses that develop in harness with it, is constitutive of the character of its object — its beauty, its goodness, its magic or spell.

I have been thinking about sexual love, which of course itself can take different forms. and I have been concerned with the way it goes beyond what is biological and instinctive in sexuality, although what constitutes it are phenomena of sexuality. I have pointed out that the character of these phenomena lies partly in their various connections with phenomena outside the domain of sexuality. We could say that phenomena which in other contexts of human life do not have a sexual significance — praise, gratitude and dedication for instance — enter into it. These phenomena here assume a sexual significance, become phenomena of sexuality, and also transform the character of the sexuality that is sexual love. Rush Rhees, in developing Wittgenstein's discussion of language, emphasized the interconnections between what Wittgenstein called 'language-games' and tried to understand the sense in which these belong to a language spoken by a people with a particular life and culture (Rhees, 1970). In a somewhat similar way sexuality is not a compartment of human life and links with other aspects of human life. A great deal that enriches it and endows it with the significance it can have in individual lives goes through much of human life. This contribution, also, is a two-way one, for it is equally true that people enter most of the things they do as sexual beings — their sexuality, like their morality, is an important part of their perspective on the world. It plays a part in determining what they can make of things in various connections of human life and what they can bring to their engagement in various practices.

I spoke of the interdependence between the phenomena of sexual love and literature (to which I should add other forms of art, especially music). The latter develops the forms of expression and sensibility which in an important sense constitute the phenomena of love, even though these obviously have a biological aspect. On the other hand, the phenomena exist independently of each individual artist and writer who, through his portrayal of various aspects of them, makes us see these aspects anew. He does not tell us what love is; he *shows* us what it is like. As Rhees puts it (1971, p. 24):

> Evidently none can write about love. Gifted writers don't try. (Stendhal — but has anyone else ?). When anyone does, the result is commonplace and boring. Not because love is boring. It is the theme of poems and plays and stories more frequently, perhaps, than any other. And a new portrayal of it by any real writer will always hold us. But if he starts to tell us *about* love, we stop reading.

Dr. Leavis makes the same point in his essay on *Anna Karenina* (1967, pp. 12–13). The book, he says,

> concerns itself everywhere. . .with the relations between men and women: love in its varieties, marriage in its varieties, the meaning of marriage. The essential mode of the book carries with it the implication that there *could* be no simple statement of a real problem, or of any 'answer' worth having. It is the very antithesis of a didactic mode. The book says in effect, 'This is life'. . .The creative writer's way of arriving at and presenting general truths about life is that which Tolstoy exemplifies with such resource. . . Only a work of art can say with validity and force, as *Anna Karenina* does, 'This is life.'

John Wisdom has compared the way art, and especially literature, reveals new aspects in things familiar and the way philosophy does so,[2] and it is well known that Wittgenstein himself distinguished between what can be said and what can only be shown, and attached great importance to this distinction in philosophy. Just as the literary writer does not try to tell us what love is, so also the philosopher ought not to try and define the concepts around which his investigations resolve. The main reason for this which Wittgenstein had in mind was that the philosopher would have to presuppose an understanding of these concepts in his inquiry into them. With this I am not now concerned. What I do want to point out is that the philosopher's problems are different from those of the literary writer, even though they may overlap. In

[2] See my discussion of his treatment of this question in Dilman, 1974a.

connection with 'the nature of love' his problems, as mine, may centre around where sexuality enters into it and in what way. Obviously Freud's treatment of sexuality and the central place he accorded to it in human life raises these problems in an acute form, and that is my reason for discussing them in the course of a critical appreciation of his thought.

The point at which I started was to note the variety in the tendencies which 'sexual love' shares with other forms of love. I broke off my presentation of this variety in order to discuss the question about the sense in which these tendencies have a sexual character and the way in which they differ from sexual desires, for instance in the case of lust, where we should not wish to speak of love. I spoke first of affection and then of being captivated by the magic, the beauty of the beloved. Love, I suggested, is a turbulent passion, one that takes possession of a person and becomes the centre of his world, changing his values and affecting his way of making sense of things. Elsewhere (Dilman, forthcoming, chapter 3) we considered the way in which emotions transform one's aware-ness of the world — vide Sartre — and the dispositions to action that are constitutive of them — vide Hampshire. Love, however, is not just one emotion among others, an emotion like any other. Otherwise why should it have been 'the theme of poems and plays and stories more frequently than any other'?

It incorporates many different emotions, tendencies and desires which vary from case to case so that we have many different forms or expressions of love in human life. I men-tioned the desire to have and to hold, to touch, to communi-cate and enter into some form of communion, to contemplate, to take delight in the person loved, to create or beget through the beloved, to give, to care, to protect, to be worthy of love. These desires and dispositions are inspired by the beauty, the magic which the beloved has in the lover's apprehension, the dearness he or she has in the lover's feeling. Love itself is perhaps better described as a mode of sensibility in which what is loved becomes an object of delight. It can be described as an attitude of will exemplified in caring and commitment. It is also a mode of relationship. Interest and admiration are others, although each of these overlaps with love and they all share some of each other's character. Love offers the possibility of intimacy, sincerity and growth. That is why its problems are the problems of human relationship and affects the meaning one can find in life. There are not comparable problems of hate for instance. A person who is unable to love is one who is unable to relate himself to things properly. Love also raises the question of whether one is worthy of what one loves.

2 Love and Creativity

What I have said so far naturally leads to two further questions. Both relate to Freud's view that all forms of love, even interest and admiration, are expressions of sexuality. First, what makes him think so and where does he go wrong in thinking this? Second, could it be, in part, because he sees in these diverse phenomena something that links them with what rejuvenates human life that he thinks of them, wrongly, as expressions of sexuality? If so, then behind his sweeping claim there may be something worth investigating.

In *Group Psychology* Freud claims that all ties between people are 'libidinal' (1949c, pp. 44—5). He then considers an objection which John Anderson was to raise in his discussion of Freud's later book *Civilization and its Discontents*: 'The question will at once be raised whether community of interest in itself, without any addition of libido, must not necessarily lead to the toleration of other people and to considerateness for them.' Freud's answer is that 'no lasting limitation of narcissism is effected in this way.' For he wrongly thinks of the 'community of interest' suggested by the objects as a form of 'rational benevolence': 'This tolerance does not persist longer than the immediate advantage gained from the other people's collaboration. . .Experience has shown that in cases of collaboration libidinal ties are regularly formed between the fellow-workers which prolong and solidify the relation between them to a point beyond what is merely profitable.' He concludes that 'love alone acts as the civilising factor in the sense that it brings a change from egoism to altruism' (Freud, 1949c, p. 57). In *Civilization and its Discontents* he writes: 'The masses of men must be bound to one another libidinally; necessity alone, the advantages of common work, would not hold them together' (1949f, p. 102).

Anderson criticizes Freud's idea of libido being necessary to the co-operation between men (1940, p. 347): 'Man is *not* confronted with the task of living with his fellows, but is social all along.' Being social, men '*are* held together in common work'. It is not 'the advantages of common work' that hold men together, but 'the common work itself' (Anderson, 1940, p. 345). I shall return to Anderson's criticisms of Freud's individualism in chapter 6. What I should like to point out here is that love is a mode of relationship, not the only one, but the earliest. It is in the course of the development of love that a child learns to control his immediate impulses, to relate to and co-operate with others, notably his parents. What he thus learns enables him to learn other modes of relationship, such as the joint pursuit of common interests, and it is carried over into them. This is what Malinowski has in mind when he says that 'common sociability develops by extension of the family bonds' (1955, p. 165). It is true that 'man is not confronted with the task of living with his fellows'. But only because most men are on the whole co-operative, are interested in things and pursue their interests in common activities. Anderson is quite right in thinking that these interests come from outside and presuppose the existence of a social life. To have them is to be part of that life. Without them, if we also include men's values, there would be little on which to co-operate. However, if men are capable of co-operating with each other, capable of learning and of becoming part of the life of a community, this is because of their early experiences in their family. If they do not develop the ability to love and co-operate, then living with their fellows becomes a task and a problem. Freud thinks that these two abilities are intimately interrelated: 'love. . .brings a change from egoism to altruism.' By 'altruism' he means interest in other people and concern for their welfare.

These do indeed form part of our conception of love — which does not mean that love cannot be selfish, nor that there cannot be co-operation without love. It is well known that men who actually dislike each other often co-operate when it is in their interest to do so. But even when they do not pretend to like each other there is a strain: 'No lasting

limitation of narcissism is effected in this way.' However, in
the absence of positive dislike for one another men do generally co-operate, and what brings this about is common work,
common interest, common values; not interest in each other.
Freud recognizes this and speaks of 'identification' as a special
kind of relation in contrast with what he calls 'object choice'.
He says that here a number of individuals share a common
'ego ideal', i.e. look up to and admire the same person or are
inspired by the same values and ideals, and consequently
'identify themselves with one another in their ego' (Freud,
1949c, p. 80). As he puts it: 'A soldier takes his superior. . .as
his ideal, while he identifies himself with his equals' (1949c,
p. 111). In *Civilization and its Discontents* too he contrasts
'sexual love' and 'identification': 'The conflict between
civilization and sexuality is caused by the circumstance that
sexual love is a relationship between two people, in which a
third can only be superfluous or disturbing, whereas civilisation is founded on relations between larger groups of persons.'
In these larger groups men are tied together by 'powerful
identifications' (1949f, pp. 79–80). However, he seems to
think of both as 'libidinal ties'.

Compare and contrast with D. H. Lawrence writing on the
same question (1977, pp. 109–10):

> Is this new polarity, this new circuit of passion between comrades
> and co-workers, is this also sexual?. . .
>
> This meeting of many in one great passionate purpose is not
> sex, and should never be confused with sex. It is a great motion in
> the opposite direction. . .When man loses his deep sense of pur-
> posive, creative activity, he feels lost, and is lost. When he makes
> the sexual consummation the supreme consummation, even in his
> *secret* soul, he falls into the beginnings of despair. . .
>
> The great collective passion of belief which brings men together,
> comrades and co-workers. . .this is not sex-passion. . .Sex holds
> any *two* people together, but it tends to disintegrate society,
> unless it is subordinated to the great dominating male passion of
> collective *purpose*.

Lawrence is saying that sex or what Freud calls 'eros' is not
the only 'life force' or 'constructive principle' in human life.
There is another principle at work in men's lives which has an

important contribution to make to the meaning of their lives. This is what Freud calls 'common ego-ideal'. Lawrence and Freud disagree about its character.

The term Lawrence uses for it, 'collective purpose', covers a range of phenomena. He has in mind friendships inspired by common ideals, comradeships that develop through participation in common activities, the tie between colleagues who belong to the same profession, the regard for each other of people fighting for the same cause. His term 'passion of belief' is more accurate, though by 'purpose' I take him to mean that such passion gives purpose to men's lives in the sense of 'direction' or 'orientation'. There is no implication that the direction in question is that of means to an end. I agree with Lawrence; I see no reason for characterizing such ties as 'sexual' or 'libidinal'. I also agree with his characterization of what is at work here as a 'passion'. What he calls 'passion of belief' is devotion to an ideal, loyalty to a cause, dedication of the self to a value.[3] These are phenomena of love — with an important qualification.

People can be brought together by a common enemy; they can be held together by sharing what Erikson calls 'negative identities' — by hating the same things, having contempt for the same values. These are not phenomena of love, although friendship may grow between people who have come together in this way. If this happens, the friendship may transform their hatred. Secondly, whether or not devotion to an ideal is a phenomenon of love depends on the ideal and can be seen in what it is capable of inspiring in men who devote themselves to it. But, by and large, men's devotions to positive ideals have involved some measure of love.

I think that Freud was right in distinguishing between sexual love on the one hand and admiration and identification on the other. He saw both of these beginning to develop in the child's relationships with members of his family. He thought that in these beginnings we have the precursor of the great variety which phenomena of love take in adult life. Critics were right in emphasizing how much that is new comes

---

[3] This is what is meant by a 'belief in' a value or ideal. I discuss this question in Dilman, 1979, and I shall return to it in chapter 5 below.

into adult life from *outside*; how much what a person learns from his participation in the life that goes on around him and his contact with those sharing it *transforms* the character of what comes from his childhood. On the other hand Freud is right in thinking that the kind of relationships a person can enter into, what he can make of them and what he can learn depend on what he brings to these. The most important part of what he brings to them dates back to his childhood and includes the kind of love of which he is capable. His capacity for contact, co-operation and creativity springs from it.

We have seen that men can co-operate with one another in a limited way out of self-interest. A deeper co-operation takes love and friendship, or a common interest or concern. I suggested that the latter also are phenomena of love or have some affinity to such phenomena. Ian D. Suttie, one of the critics of the central importance which Freud attaches to sexuality, indicates the affinity succinctly. After noting the way the growing child's widening environment replaces the world of which his mother occupies the centre, he continues (Suttie, 1948, p. 16):

> A joint interest in *things* has replaced the reciprocal interest in *persons*; friendship has developed out of love. True, the personal love and sympathy is preserved in *friendship*; but this differs from love insofar as it comes about by the *direction of attention upon the same things* (rather than upon each other), or by the pursuit of *the same activities*. . .The interest is intensified even if it is not entirely created. . .by being *shared*; while the fact of sharing interest deepens the appreciation of the other person's presence even while it deprives it of sensual. . .qualities.

Of course love can be selfish, it can introduce strife and conflict between people – strife and conflict which would not be there but for love. For although generosity and concern are expressions of love, it is also true that love can be the source of demands which the lover makes on the beloved – demands for what ideally the beloved is willing to give unsolicited as part of her love. I am thinking of sexual love, but this is equally true of friendship. Thus the lover desires that his love should be returned, and the friend that his friendship should be reciprocated. This is part of sexual love and of friendship, and there is nothing selfish in this desire as such. But when it turns into need the demands that issue from it become expressions of selfishness. This selfishness was in the lover before he fell in love and his love becomes the vehicle of his selfishness. But in doing so it becomes selfish itself; the desire which is an expression of love and belongs to it takes on a selfish character. Given its common occurrence it can be described as one form of love. Thus we sometimes speak of 'selfish love', 'possessive love', 'destructive love', 'dependent love', and so on.

In view of this variety, are we to say that the connection I hinted at between love and the capacity to give and take and to co-operate is purely gratuitous? I do not think so. I said that the phenomena of love are various and can be classified in different ways. One distinction one can make within this variety is this: in some cases we have love which is directed to a particular person on account of who he is. We can describe it as 'selective' or 'personal' because it chooses its object. Thus in maternal love a mother loves her child because the child is her offspring, because she has brought him into the world, nursed and cared for him. In sexual love the lover loves the beloved because of whatever it is in her that inspires this passion in him. If and when this passion is consolidated with affection, common memories and shared experiences will add a new dimension to the particularity of the beloved. It is in some ways the same with friendship. In contrast, compassion or what Christians call 'love of one's neighbour' is not selective in this way — for everyone without exception is one's neighbour in this sense. It is the same with a person's belief in, loyalty and devotion to certain moral values. The practices which embody these values do not differentiate between one person and another. In these latter cases the values themselves give us a measure for distinguishing between pure and impure forms of their love, between genuine compassion and its corrupt varieties. Hence Simone Weil characterizes compassion as love of justice.

We can, of course, do the same in the case of those phenomena of love which are 'selective' in the sense indicated. Thus Simone Weil on friendship: 'All friendship is impure if even a trace of the wish to please, or the contrary desire to dominate is found in it' (1959, p. 157). Similarly for sexual love and affection: 'When the bonds of affection and necessity between human beings are not supernaturally transformed into friendship, not only is the affection of an impure and low order, but it is also combined with hatred and repulsion. That is shown very well in *L'École des Femmes* and in *Phèdre*' (Weil, 1959, p. 159). One problem concerns the compatibility between sexual love (what she calls 'carnal love') and friendship. Simone Weil is well aware of this problem: 'The essential thing about love is that it consists in a vital need that one human being feels for another. . .Because of this the problem is to reconcile this need with the equally imperious need for freedom; this is a problem that men have wrestled with since time immemorial' (Weil, 1951, p. 35). When writing about friendship she refers to this 'need for freedom' as the need to 'respect the distance which the fact of being two distinct creatures places between them', i.e. between the friends (Weil, 1959, p. 157). Her problem there is to show how friendship, which is necessarily 'personal', *can* be 'supernatural' and, therefore, pure: 'Friendship is a miracle by which a person consents to view from a certain distance, and without coming any nearer, the very being who is necessary to him as food' (p. 157). It 'has in it, at the same time as affection, something not unlike a complete indifference. Although it is a bond between two people it is in a sense impersonal' (p. 158). The problem with sexual love and passion is whether it can view the beloved from a distance in this way, whether it can assume this kind of 'impersonality' and 'indifference', without stopping to be what it is.

My problem is a different one, namely whether there is an inherent connection between love and generosity, between love and creativeness, between love and the capacity to cooperate. This is a problem in view of the fact that love *itself* can be selfish, destructive and tyrannical. But to speak of an 'inherent connection' here is not to claim that love is always generous, that it can never be selfish; it is not to deny that love can bring out the worst in a man as well as the best. To deny this would be to deny that love offers problems and that struggling with these problems is the kind of growth which love brings into human life. Thus to claim that there is an inherent connection between love and generosity is to claim that a love that is selfish necessarily has certain tensions within it, so that a person who loves selfishly can reconcile himself to it only through self-deception. Again love, sexual love, is captivating; in it the lover falls a prey to the magic of the beloved. Being the way he is his love may take a dependent form. He may resent this and hate the beloved for it. The hatred here does not, of course, belong to the love, so that the conflict we have is not one between different parts of the love in question. However, this dependency could easily come into conflict, given the right circumstances, with the lover's concern for the beloved and his desire to be worthy of her love. He would then see it as something of which he wishes to purge his love. If he describes his love as a 'low' form of love the measure of his condemnation comes from love itself. Here the disposition to care for the beloved which the lover has by virtue of his love will be in conflict with his need for and dependence on the beloved. Where that disposition changes into a 'commitment of will' the lover will view his dependence as a weakness and feel unworthy. Here then we have a form of love which has within it the principle of its development.

I am suggesting that although love for another person can take many different forms and can become a vehicle for the expression of what is good and bad, constructive and destructive in human beings, they are not all on an equal footing. In grasping some of these as forms of love we see them as variants of other forms, variants in which tendencies that are expressions of love *par excellence* as warped or distorted by the idiosyncrasies of both the lover and the beloved. We understand that love can go these ways because we understand what love is and know what human life is like. Thus love could not be jealous and possessive were the beloved not precious to the lover; and one individual becoming precious to another is part of what we understand by love. The jealousy and possessiveness are not necessary to love and come from idiosyncrasies of the people in love, but that they should be precious to each other is necessary, although this can take many different forms. Again, while love can take a selfish form or be exacting in particular cases, generosity is an expression of love, selfishness is not. By generosity I understand the ability to give and share willingly and without any condition.

Love can be harsh and cruel, but cruelty and harshness are the contribution of the idiosyncrasies of the lover and the circumstances of his love. They are the expression which his love takes in these circumstances, but we cannot speak of them as expressions of love as such. Compassion on the other hand is an expression of love. By compassion I understand feeling sorry for those who are hurt, deprived of what they need, and suffering. Its counterpart, where there is no hurt, is sympathy, that is, the ability to enter into another person's concerns, interests and joys. It makes it possible for the other person to share these with one. That is why it is sometimes said that love brings understanding or that it is discerning. But it is also well known that love can be blind and bring illusion. The blindness and the illusion come from other aspects of love, from desire and wishful thinking.

Again, love can be unforgiving; but it takes love both to forgive and to feel grateful. Generosity concerns not only the spirit in which a person gives, but also that in which he receives what he is given. A person who has no love in his heart will see no reason for thanking anyone. He may thank someone out of expediency or politeness, but he will not feel grateful. It takes love not only to feel sorry for those in pain and to forgive those who have wronged one, but also to feel guilty and remorseful for the wrong one has done to others. Thus forgiveness, gratitude, compassion, sympathy, grief, guilt and remorse are all expressions of love, in the sense that they are responses which presuppose love.

This is true also of trust. Love, of course, need not be trusting — hence Marcel's suspicions of Albertine. But where there is no love there can be no trust, only the judgement that a particular person is reliable or honest. For there is a difference between trusting that a machine will not break down and will accomplish a particular task and putting one's faith in another person, trusting that he will not let one down. Such an act of faith involves both judgement and generosity. For in trusting someone not only is one of the opinion that he is trustworthy, but one is willing to put oneself in his hands, to speak and answer for him. This is taking a risk and thus an act of faith in this sense is an act of love. Loyalty is closely connected with it: it is a response to what in the other inspires one's trust. It means that one is prepared to stand by him in adversity, stick one's neck out for him, defend him. Patience, too, which is the suffering of wrong without complaint and without attempting to repay the wrongdoer for it, takes love. It presupposes a loving attitude. So does accepting a person with his shortcomings and weaknesses. For it is easy enough to associate with and like someone who is pleasant, interesting, charming and enjoyable. This involves little giving or putting oneself out. The test of love is whether one can take him with his faults, carry his burdens.

We see that despite its great diversity of forms and faces we can still say that love is a mode of affectivity. Where it goes deep it is also a mode of will which finds its centre outside the self. From that centre the lover derives sustenance, paradoxically, not by what he takes but by what he gives of himself. He is enriched by this giving. What he receives from the other person is not what he takes, it is a gift. If we say that this is what love is like 'in an ideal world', then we should remember the way our application of the concepts of pure geometry and theoretical physics helps us to understand the world in which we live. We can still understand what love is like 'in the real world' best if we can relate instances of it to what it is like when the tendencies and dispositions that belong to it are 'pure and unadulterated'[4] For we can see the variety of forms these assume in the special circumstances of human life. It would not be too difficult to find a place for what Freud calls 'secondary narcissism' among the many forms of love; but this is not so easy with his 'primary narcissism'. Perhaps it is a taking on, on the part of the young child, of a doting mother's affective attitude towards him — a form of identification with her.

If I am right about the inherent connection between love and generosity, then its creative character flows from this connection. Thus contrast any number of attitudes and emotions such as hatred, resentment and envy with love. These will direct and fix a man's actions and life on certain targets and objectives, as when he nurses a grudge or is bent

---

[4] Thus I find no incompatability between this kind of Platonism and Wittgenstein's anti-essentialism. See Dilman, 1980, chapter 10, section V.

on revenge, which will prevent anything new entering his life. Generally the response which these will evoke in others will perpetuate these attitudes and add to the staleness of such a life. With love, however it is awakened, we have the possibility of something new entering into and renewing that life. For instance, he may be able to forgive his adversaries, find that he can respond to them in new ways, enter into their ways of thinking in a way he could never do before. This may change his relationship to his adversaries into a moving thing and also broaden his horizons. Or he may give up craving for everything he does not have, seeking to spoil it for others and annexing it to himself. Doing so never enriched him, never mitigated the sense of deprivation that drove him to it. Now no longer treating things, including other people's qualities and achievements, as what only he must be allowed to enjoy, he has for the first time the opportunity to see them for what they are. Consequently he may not want some of them and be happy to allow those who do to enjoy them. He will, in turn, be able to enjoy the things he has and even to add to them.

This is also true of grief, guilt and remorse. They are sometimes regarded as what arrests the flow of life. If someone grieves or feels remorse this obviously means that he cares about the person he has lost or hurt, feeling bad about being the bearer of the harm he had done him. What arrests his life is not what he feels, but what he has lost or what he has done. If he did not care his life would go on as before; but it would not have been the life we imagined, one in which love and affection for a particular person held an important place. The flow of his life would not have been arrested, but it would have been the flow of a much flatter life. This would be equally true if he were a man who did not care about cheating a stranger, telling a lie, or letting a friend down. If, on the other hand, he did care about these things but was gradually led to neglect them, then remorse, however painful, would be a return to caring for these things. It would arrest the flow of a life that has become stagnant with indifference to these values. At the end of *Crime and Punishment* Dostoyevsky shows very clearly how the arrest by remorse and repentance of his earlier schemes is a thawing out of much that was frozen in Raskolnikov's life and heart. I am suggesting that grieving and mourning for the loss of a loved person *is* something creative, in contrast with not allowing oneself to feel pain. The same is true of remorse and repentance.

On the other side of love we have put indifference, which allows selfishness to grow rampant, and hatred, which is a response to anyone who stands in the way of such selfishness. Hatred, resentment and envy, when we say of a person that he is 'eaten up' with these things, prevent gratuitous contact with the outer world and starve man's spirit. They drive a person to the pursuit of their objectives and narrow his contact to the orbit of their requirement. Of course, love too can drive a person in this way when it is possessive and jealous, and in its obsessive forms it too will come between him and the world's offerings. But what we are dealing with here are needs that stem from feelings of persecution and deprivation of the self, lack of faith in others and the inability to trust them. It is these that shape and twist the love in question, even when they become the vehicle through which love finds expression.

When love is free from such fear and anxiety, when it is purged of the needs of the self, it can be itself and bring generosity into a man's life, and thought for other people. Regard for their good can thus come to have a firm place among the sources that inspire action. It also brings a new kind of responsibility into that life, such that a man feels sympathy and concern for others, feels sorry if he has done them harm, is pained if he lets down his friends. The many aspects of the meaning of the word 'care' in our language reflects what I am trying to bring together. For to care is to look after, to nurse and to nurture. It is also the opposite of indifference in a special way: if I care for something then I shall be concerned for its well-being in such a way that anything that hurts that well-being will hurt me. Consequently I will do my utmost to provide conditions that favour its development, protect it, grieve when it is damaged, attempt to restore it. This is obviously creative if the opposite of creativeness is either destructiveness or so insulating things that nothing will change them. I have suggested that love is creative in that it exposes one's life to contact with what lies outside it so that it remains mobile and growing. It is creative in contrast with attitudes that come from hatred, greed and selfishness. These turn the spirit inwards and keep it circling around the same spot. It is creative in its power to diminish selfishness and mitigate hatred. The fact that a person's love can be selfish or destructive does not show that it does not have this power.

I think that Melanie Klein would agree with much of what I have said about the creative character of love. One of the central tenets of her thought is that creativeness is the prerogative of a life that is built around loving relationships. Its foundations are laid in very early childhood (See Klein, 1960, pp. 6–7). In her discussions of 'envy and gratitude', 'love, guilt and reparation', 'grief and depression', and the child's attempts to avoid feeling these, 'the manic defense', it is clear that she thinks of love as playing a central role in the growth of the child.

What is striking is the change of perspective from Freud to Melanie Klein. Freud considered the child's development largely from the point of view of his struggle for independence from cravings, often encouraged by his mother, which bring him in conflict with his father – a struggle which reaches its climax with the crystallization of the Oedipus complex. Melanie Klein, on the other hand, while not ignoring this, placed greater emphasis on the child's struggle with his own destructiveness and the fears stemming from it – fears both about himself and about those he depends upon and loves. Thus she speaks of 'the constant interaction of love and hate' in the life of the young child. She still speaks of 'love' and 'libido' interchangeably, almost by habit, but it is clear that she takes a wider conception of love than Freud did. This, as we shall see in chapters 4 and 5, makes for a great difference in their respective treatment of the phenomena of morality.

My main criticism of Freud in this chapter has been concerned with the way he ties up love with sexuality. Failing to recognize that love can have an identity independent from sexuality, he does not appreciate the contribution of love to a relationship when it is one with sexuality, the way it transforms that sexuality. As Guntrip puts it (1949, p. 237): 'Instinct theory interprets personality and its phases of growth by sex. A truly human and personal psychology will interpret sex by the part it plays in the personal life and the process of integration.'

4

Morality and the Individual

1 Freud's Estimate of Morality

In a letter to Einstein 'Why War?' in 1932, Freud begins by giving an account of how considerations of what is right have come to weigh with us (1950, vol. v, p. 274): 'To-day right and violence appear to us as antitheses. It can easily be shown, however, that the one has developed out of the other.' His account is very similar to the one given by Callicles in Plato's *Gorgias* (483). The original state of things consisted of the 'domination by whoever had the greater might'. But 'this regime was altered in the course of evolution'. Freud asks: 'What was the path that led from violence to right or law?' He answers: 'The path that led by way of the fact that the superior strength of a single individual could be rivalled by the union of several weak ones.' He goes on: 'The power of those who were united now represented law in contrast to the violence of the single individual.' He concludes: 'Right is the might of a community. It is still violence...it works by the same methods and follows the same purposes. The only real difference lies in the fact that what prevails is no longer the violence of an individual but that of a community' (p. 275). He then asks what psychological condition must be fulfilled for this transition to take place. He answers that 'the union of the majority must be a stable and lasting one.' What makes it so? 'The growth of emotional ties between the members of a united group of people — feelings of unity which are the true source of its strength' (p. 276). Freud does not share Callicles' contempt for the majority; but apart from that difference what he says about the emotional ties that unite a group is the only substantial addition he makes to Callicles' account. In *Group Psychology* he discusses the nature of these emotional ties and the way they hold together the members of the group.

Here we have the germ of Freud's idea of morality as consisting of external precepts and sanctions imposed upon the individual — 'imposed' because they are at variance with man's nature. The implication is that if it were possible for man to be 'left to himself', if he had the courage to be himself, he would not heed the precepts of morality. For man does not adhere to morality willingly.

In *The Future of an Illusion* (first published in 1927) and *Civilization and its Discontents* (first published in 1930), Freud is not very far from the idea that moral beliefs are an illusion: 'Having recognized religious doctrines to be illusions, we are at once confronted with the further question: may not other cultural possessions, which we esteem highly and by which we let our life be ruled, be of a similar nature?' (Freud, 1949e, p. 59). Of course, if one claims them to be illusions, one can then go on to ask: How come that men believe them? How does it come about that men submit themselves to the claims of morality? In this way logical room is made for a psychological account, for a 'moral psychology'.

In Freud's case we have his doctrine of the formation of the super-ego: culture and morality are built on coercion and instinctual renunciation. Men, in their childhood, take over this external compulsion and conform to the precepts of morality conveyed to them by their parents. That part of themselves which does the compelling is the super-ego (Freud, 1949f, pp. 106—8):

> Since their own feelings would not have led men along the same path, they must have had a motive for obeying this extraneous influence. It is easy to discover this motive in men's helplessness and dependence upon others; it can best be designated the dread of losing love. . .Because of the dread of this loss, one must desist from it — viz. from what is bad, from whatever causes one to be threatened with a loss of love. . . .At this stage the sense of guilt is obviously only the dread of losing love, 'social' anxiety. . .[This]

anxiety relates only to the possibility of detection. . .A great
change takes place as soon as the authority has been internalized
by the development of a super-ego. At this point the dread of
discovery ceases to operate and also. . .any difference between
doing evil and wishing to do it, since nothing is hidden from the
super-ego.

Despite this 'great change', however, the claims of morality
remain *external* to the individual's will, the super-ego remains
divided from the ego. For the individual has still to compel
himself to conform to the demands of morality and does so
to avoid punishment in the hands of a harsh super-ego, i.e.
to avoid the pangs of a bad conscience. These pangs, according
to Freud, are the individual's 'aggressiveness' turned inwards
(1949f, p. 105):

> What means does civilisation make use of to hold in check the
> aggressiveness that opposes it. . .? What happens in him [the
> individual] to render his craving for aggression innocuous?. . .The
> aggressiveness is introjected, 'internalised'; in fact, it is sent back
> where it came from, i.e. directed against the ego. It is there taken
> over by a part of the ego that distinguishes itself from the rest as
> a super-ego, and now, in the form of 'conscience', exercises the
> same propensity to harsh aggressiveness against the ego that the
> ego would have liked to enjoy against others.

The implication remains that the individual is not capable
of caring and showing consideration for others, of feeling
sympathy for them, rejoicing at their good fortune and
sorrowing at their misery, and of feeling bad if he hurts them
himself — capable of these things 'on his own account' and
not because he is made to do so by an external or internal
agency. Freud is not entirely unequivocal on this point. In
his paper 'Thoughts for the Times of War and Death' (1915)
he touches on this question. In the first part of that paper he
speaks of the disillusionment brought by the behaviour of
states and individuals during war (1950, vol. iv, p. 295):

> Two things in this war have evoked our sense of disillusionment:
> the destitution shown in moral relations externally by the states
> which in their interior relations pose as the guardians of accepted

moral usage, and the brutality in behaviour shown by individuals, whom, as partakers in the highest form of human civilisation, one would not have credited with such a thing.

He argues that this disillusionment is not justified — 'for it consists in the destruction of an illusion' (p. 294).

Let us be clear that what he characterizes as an illusion here is our belief in human beings not, as in *The Future of an Illusion*, our belief in the values of a morality of love. His reason for doing so is this: 'In reality, there is no such thing as "eradicating" evil tendencies' (p. 295). He says: 'The inmost essence of human nature consists of elemental instincts, which are common to all men. . .These instincts in themselves are neither good nor evil. We but classify them and their manifestations in that fashion, according as they meet the needs and demands of the human community' (p. 295). This last point fits in with the line he takes in his letter to Einstein that 'right is the might of a community'. Freud admits that 'these primitive instincts undergo a lengthy process of development' (p. 296). He is here answering the question, 'How do we imagine the process by which an individual attains to a higher plane of morality?' (p. 295). But what kind of development is this? Freud is pulled in two different directions. On the one hand he wants to say that these instincts can be 'transformed', although he rightly qualifies this: 'we are. . . misled by our optimism into grossly exaggerating the number of human beings who have been transformed in a civilised sense' (p. 299). It is this inflated belief about human beings which he earlier characterized as an illusion. On the other hand he is also inclined to think not just that such a transformation is rare, but that it is impossible: 'These primitive instincts. . .are inhibited, directed towards other aims and departments, become comingled, alter their objects, and are to some extent turned back upon their possessor. Reaction-formations against certain instincts take the deceptive form of a change in content, as though egoism had changed into altruism, or cruelty into pity' (p. 296). The suggestion is that such a change is more apparent than real: 'The primitive mind is, in the fullest meaning of the word, imperishable' (p. 301).

There is truth in what Freud claims here. The hatred and propensity to destructiveness that an individual may have had in him and intensified in his early childhood may well remain with him all his life. If he is fortunate and it is actually diminished by his later experiences, it may still leave a sediment of proneness to bad temper and suspicion in his later life. Melanie Klein who, as we shall see later, does believe in the possibility of a genuine transformation of the individual in this respect, agrees with Freud (Klein, 1948, p. 73): 'Psycho-analysis cannot altogether do away with man's aggressive instinct as such.' But even when this early propensity to destructiveness remains with a man, it does not make him incapable of genuinely caring for others, it does not decrease his capacity to act nobly – that is, from noble motives. On the contrary, part of his nobility lies in the way he overcomes this propensity in himself. When Freud says that these instincts or propensities are in themselves neither good nor evil he means that whether or not they are so depends on what the man does with them, the kind of action into which they enter.

I said that on the whole Freud is right in thinking that people's morality is only skin-deep, at any rate that it does not go very deep with most people. On this point Simone Weil would agree with him, although their moral attitude to this fact is very different. Freud is 'pessimistic', while Simone Weil can love and hope for human beings in a way that is alien to Freud's 'scientific' attitude. Freud is right in thinking that morality is something that comes to the individual from outside and that in the course of his moral development it has to work its way downward, as it were, penetrate what is deeper, conquer what is most intimate in him. In this process of assimilation and civilization, the individual has to give up some things, he has to learn self-mastery. Freud's view is that on the whole this process does not go deep with people (1950, vol. iv, p. 301): 'Whenever we sleep we cast off our hard-won morality like a garment, only to put it on again next morning.' I do not think that this shows that our morality is not genuine or is superficial, and in what Freud says about it he contradicts his earlier claim that 'these instincts in themselves are neither good nor evil'. For our dreams show that we have such propensities, but not that we are indifferent to having them. It is different with our behaviour in waking life. Though even here our behaviour in extreme conditions is not enough to show how deep our morality goes.

Freud mentions one particular situation: the way the individual lowers his sights and standards when those around him seem to find this acceptable, for instance, during wartime. He discusses this question in connection with the psychology of crowds and recognizes that what we have here is a special phenomenon in which the individual relinquishes his responsibility for his actions. In *Group Psychology* he compares it with hypnotic suggestibility where a person puts his will in commission, lends or entrusts it to the safekeeping of another person. A man who is caught up in a crowd sinks his individuality; and his morality, if it is genuine and not mere conformity, is what distinguishes him as an individual. What was impossible to contemplate for him now becomes possible. Freud, who makes penetrating observations on this phenomenon in *Group Psychology*, draws the wrong conclusion both there and in his reflections on war: 'We can find no difficulty in understanding the disappearance of conscience. . .It has long been our contention that "dread of society" is the essence of what is called conscience' (Freud, 1949c, p. 10). 'It cannot be a matter for astonishment. . .that this relaxation of all the moral ties between the greater units of mankind should have a seducing influence on the morality of individuals; for our conscience. . .in its origin is "dread of the community" and nothing else. When the community has no rebuke to make, there is an end of all suppression of the baser passions' (Freud, 1950, vol. iv, p. 294).

Obviously where a man's moral behaviour is conditioned by the fear of his fellow-men's disapproval, if that disapproval is suspended he will cease to behave as he has done so far. It follows that the behaviour was not genuinely moral, inspired not by moral considerations but by considerations of the self — prudence, expediency or fear. This need not be the case, however, and the individual may be seduced into abandoning something that is genuine — as by hypnosis. Freud recognizes this and he speaks of regression (1950, vol. iv, p. 302): 'Undoubtedly the influences of war are among the forces that can bring about such regression.' He further acknowledges that what one regresses from need not be anything less real than what one regresses to: 'Therefore we need not deny adaptability for culture to all who are at the present time displaying uncivilised behaviour, and we may anticipate that the refinement of their instincts will be restored in times of peace' (p. 302). In other words the saying *in vino veritas* does not apply here, or need not do so. In going along with the crowd the individual need not be doing what he has always wanted to do, but for his conscience. As Freud quotes from Le Bon's *La Psychologie des Foules*: 'He is no longer conscious of his acts. . .He is no longer himself, but has become an automaton who has ceased to be guided by his will' (Freud, 1949c, p. 12).

The point I am arguing is this: The fact that morality is something that comes to the individual from outside and has to work its way downward, as I put it, does not mean that it is only a veneer. The fact that a man can be caught up in a crowd and lose his morality and individuality does not show that his morality is something that he wears like a garment. It does not follow, therefore, that coming to have moral beliefs is not a genuine transformation of the individual. A deep transformation may be rare, but that does not make it impossible. Freud says that 'when a village grows into a town. . .the village. . .becomes submerged in the town'. Here, he says, 'the old materials or forms have been superseded and replaced by new ones'. But, he claims, 'it is otherwise with the development of the mind' (1950, vol. iv, p. 301). I have agreed that there is truth in Freud's claim; but it is only a half truth. It may indeed be true that 'every earlier stage of development persists alongside the later stage', but it is not true that the later stage has simply 'developed from' the earlier stages, so that the individual acquires nothing that is new, nothing that was not already contained in him from the start. The language that he learns to speak, the way this enables him to think, to take part in and make sense of activities that go on around him, the social heritage that it makes accessible to him, this alone makes a momentous difference to his life. It has the power to transform it into something altogether different. A whole range of sentiments, moral and otherwise, becomes possible for him. They can become his, part of his experience as an individual. Thus if in the course of his moral development the individual has to give up something, which he may not give up completely, we should not forget that he also comes to possess what he did not and could not have had before.

Furthermore, if morality comes to the individual from outside, this does not mean that it can only be something imposed upon him, something that must remain external to his will. For it is equally true that it works its way down, is assimilated, because it meets in the child or awakens in him propensities, natural, matter-of-course reactions which welcome it. In this way the growing child makes the morality of his parents *his own*.[1] More than imitation and identification are at work here, although both are important. This is one of the weaknesses of Freud's theory of the super-ego, and I shall return to it in the following chapter. As Jung puts it (1953, p. 26): 'Morality was not brought down on tables of stone from Sinai and imposed on the people, but is a function of the human soul, as old as humanity itself. Morality is not imposed from outside; we have it in ourselves from the start.' He is right when he says that 'of this the Freudian school must be reminded.' We shall see, presently, that Melanie Klein and her followers do not need to be reminded of this.

In Freud's view the two most basic polarities in man's life are 'eros' and 'aggression', or what comes from 'the death instinct'. Eros is what gives life. Freud calls it 'the life instinct'. In his letter to Einstein he says that he uses the term 'eros' in the sense that Plato meant it in the *Symposium* (1950, vol. iv, p. 280). In the previous chapter I criticized him for not doing so. But if he is right, it is a noteworthy fact that he does not see the life instinct or love as co-operating with what comes from outside in the name of morality. It is aggression that he sees in this role, not love. Conscience is aggression turned back on the self; it treats the ego with the same harshness the ego would like to exercise on others (See Freud, 1949f, p. 105). This is part of Freud's view of morality as something negative, as a restrictive force directed against the individual. Later a part of the individual sides with it, in its name renouncing

[1] He can, of course, later criticize it, alter it, and even reject it for different values.

what he would dearly like to do. He does so by putting at its disposal not his love, but his aggressiveness. No wonder Ernest Jones contrasts an attitude of love with a moral attitude.[2] No wonder Freud describes the changes that take place in the course of the individual's moral development largely in terms of reaction-formations: 'Reaction-formations against certain instincts take the deceptive form of a change in content, as though egoism had changed into altruism, or cruelty into pity' (1950, vol. iv, p. 296). These are, of course, defensive measures, and the individual resorts to them out of fear – originally the fear of coercion and punishment which morality represents to him, and secondarily the fear of the super-ego and its persecution of the self.

These, however, are pathological or quasi-pathological phenomena of morality, even if they may be quite common. The point I should like to make is that if the transgressions, actual or merely contemplated, for which the super-ego punishes the ego are *moral* transgressions, then it must see them as such. If it does not, as it might not, then at least the conception of a moral transgression must exist in the society to which the individual belongs. In that conception a moral transgression cannot simply be something that happens to be punishable, something that attracts moral hostility. For what, on such a view, would moral hostility be in contrast with any other form of hostility or adversity? It follows that the 'pathological' phenomena, however widespread they may be, presuppose the reality of the non-pathological phenomena of morality and can only be understood with reference to them.

There can, of course, be a form of morality in which fear and awe have a dominant position. Perhaps the morality of the Old Testament was such. But in such a morality the fear and awe would themselves have a moral character, and no individual could experience them who did not already share the understanding that belongs to that morality. We could say that it is not the fear in question that makes such a morality possible, but the other way around. Allegiance to the morality comes logically first, and the fear of transgression comes second to it. If an individual who has made the beliefs

[2] See Jones, 1937. I comment on Jones's paper in Dilman, forthcoming, chapter 11.

of such a morality his own refrained from contravening its injunctions in fear and trembling, he would *not* be doing so defensively. He would be afraid 'for his soul', afraid of what would happen to him *morally* if he disobeyed. This could not be reduced to a 'fear of castration' — though it could be represented in terms of pictures of physical punishment.[3] Freud speaks of 'moral anxiety', but this is not the same thing as what he calls 'dread of society', that is the fear of losing other people's love, of being rejected by them. Unless one is speaking of *moral* rejection. But that presupposes a prior understanding of that for which one is rejected as, for instance, a shameful act. One must think of those who reject one as seeing what one has done as shameful, base or despicable. The pain in such a rejection lies in what it conveys to one about one's deed and so about oneself. One finds this painful because one cares about certain values and standards of behaviour. If one feared transgressing certain moral demands simply because it would lead to one's rejection by others, this would not be *moral* fear, it would not amount to 'moral anxiety'.

The young child is taught this significance, made to grasp it, by the way he is punished for instance, by the explanations he is given about why he is punished. Until he is brought to see and care about what these explanations and the punishment itself are intended to convey to him, his fearful anticipation of such punishment when he does something similar in the future cannot amount to guilt. The formation of the super-ego cannot, therefore, simply consist of the internalization of parental authority. It must also involve the internalization of parental conceptions and understanding — except that 'internalization' is a misnomer here.

2 The 'Ambivalent' Character of Freud's Estimate

We are in a better position now to see why Freud took an 'ambivalent' view of morality. One could say that, paradoxically, he had at one and the same time a low opinion of both

---

[3] Hence Christian conceptions of hell in terms of 'fire and brimstone'.

men and morality. I say 'paradoxically' because in order to
have a low opinion of men one must have a high regard for
honesty, for loyalty to truth. He had high standards of duty
to his family; he admired seriousness, devotion to work and
integrity. He thought that self-mastery is 'the highest achievement which is attainable by any human being' (Puner, 1959,
p. 199). Yet his characterization of what we regard as the
higher things in human life was not very complimentary
(Freud, 1933, pp. 82, 95):

> Psycho-analysis was met by illuminating criticisms to the effect
> that man is not merely a sexual being but has nobler and higher
> feelings...For us the super-ego is the representative of all moral
> restrictions, the advocate of the impulse towards perfection, in
> short it is as much as we have been able to apprehend psychologi-
> cally of what people call the 'higher' things in human life.

As much, but no more. For what do we have here but restrictions, reaction-formations, compensations, and at best idealiza-
tions! It is no wonder that Jung has complained that Freud's
is a 'psychology without the soul' (Jung, 1966, pp. 200, 263).

This negativist view of morality in Freud was a result of
the combination of several factors:

1 In his theoretical speculations Freud was caught up in
philosophical problems to which he responded in ways we are
familiar with in the history of philosophy. Here I would
mention his analysis of how considerations of right have
come to weigh with men. I would mention his view of moral
beliefs as conventions that restrain men and regulate their
conduct, and his views about the kind of justification of
which they are susceptible. I would also mention the call of
hedonism and his views concerning the relation between
reason and the emotions.
2 His concern with the neurotic and the pathological col-
oured his view of the normal.
3 It also made him sensitive to the discrepancies between
appearance and reality, between men's ideals and their actual
conduct. Under pressure from certain philosophical miscon-
ceptions he turned the difficulties he perceived into impos-
sibilities and then represented them as illusions cherished by

men: man's morality can be no more than skin-deep when it is something alien to human nature.

4 His view that there must be unconscious motives for all conduct tended to cast suspicion on even the most elevated instances of moral conduct.

Freud's main addition to the kind of philosophical view to which he subscribed is two-fold. The first concerns the nature of the ties that bind the members of a community together. He regards these ties as the source of the strength of the community whose might is the foundation of the conception of right which its members have. For right, in Freud's analysis in his letter to Einstein, is what meets the needs and demands of the community. The second addition concerns the 'internalization' of these demands by individual members of the community as children in the family, and the way the individual 'compels himself' to obey these demands by putting his own aggression at their service, i.e. by turning it inwards. I will return to this in the next chapter.

However, Freud was not unequivocal about this view of morality and the individual's relation to it. He showed better sense when he was less in the grip of abstract thinking and also when he responded to moral issues, such as those presented to him sometimes by his patients. This 'better sense' comes through in some of his more general statements as well. He was, as we have seen, pulled in two opposite directions on at least four connected issues: (a) He was not entirely happy with his view that for men to act morally they must be compelled to do so, if only by themselves, or at least that they must have a motive, must stand to gain or at least to keep something. (b) He was not entirely happy with his view that the only kind of transformation that takes place in an individual in the course of his moral development consists in his coming to restrain his asocial or anti-social tendencies, to redirect them, or to hold them in control by means of reaction-formations. (c) He was in two minds about whether in all cases where a person resorts to a mode of conduct which flouts his morality or shows no regard for it we could say that his morality was not genuine, or at least that it was shallow.

Thus in *The Future of an Illusion* he says: 'Clearly religion has performed great services for human culture. It has contributed much toward restraining the asocial instincts' (1949e, p. 65). He then goes on to ask whether it has made men happier and more moral. He answers: 'It is doubtful whether men were in general happier at a time when religious doctrines held unlimited sway than they are now; more moral they certainly were not' (p. 66). There can be two different interpretations of what Freud meant. One supports the point I wish to reinforce, the other does not. Thus he might be saying that men were not more moral then because their behaviour was no different than it is now. Or he might be saying that although their behaviour was different, in that it was more restrained, they were not more moral for this. In the latter case he would be saying that it is not restraint that makes men moral. Unfortunately, however, I think that the first interpretation is the correct one, for he goes on to speak of the 'great concessions to human instinct' made by the priests to 'keep the masses submissive to religion': 'One sinned, and then one made oblation or did penance, and then one was free to sin anew' (pp. 66–7).

Still Freud well knew the distinction between conformity and morality, between the kind of reform which pleases society and moral change (1950, vol. iv, p. 298): 'Ethical theorists class as "good" actions only those which are the outcome of good impulses. . .But society, which is practical in its aims. . .is content if a man regulates his behaviour and actions by the precepts of civilisation, and is little concerned with his motives.' Freud, who in so much of his writings found men's motive for morality in their desire for reward and in their fear of punishment, here admits that these motives may ensure that men 'will choose to "behave well" in the civilised sense of the phrase' but they do not bring about any 'ennoblement of instinct', any inner 'transformation of egoistic into altruistic inclinations'. So Freud does have a conception of such a transformation as distinct from 'reaction-formation'; he does not think that all altruism, humility and compassion are reaction-formations against egoism, arrogance and cruelty within the self.

Nevertheless he thinks that in most cases this is so and that genuine virtue is rarer than we recognize: 'Those who as children have been the most pronounced egoists may well become the most helpful and self-sacrificing members of the community; most of our sentimentalists, friends of humanity, champions of animals, have been evolved from little sadists and animal tormentors' (Freud, 1950, vol. iv, p. 296). The word 'evolved' here refers to reaction-formation: the earlier trends remain unmodified and the growing child, anxious to be accepted by his parents and by that part of himself in which he has identified himself with them, goes to great lengths in pretending to be the opposite of what he is – primarily to appease his super-ego. It is in this sense that the 'earlier stage of development persists alongside the later stage which has developed from it' (p. 301). Here the earlier trend represents what the individual is really like, and the later part is a cover – although it is part of his character.

In so far as Freud identifies morality with what is exemplified here it is not surprising that he should have a poor opinion of it. But if he did not himself have a high regard for honesty, could he have had a poor opinion of morality as he represents it? Certainly Freud did not think of honesty in the terms in which he thought of altruism and benevolence. He was well acquainted with the obstacles to honesty; yet he could say that 'it is an assumption that every man is honest, until proven otherwise' (Wortis, 1954, p. 20). Certainly Freud did not think that there can be an analysis of a man's honesty, that a man could have motives for being honest.

One last example (d) of the ambivalence I have been speaking of is to be found in the second part of Freud's reflections on war and death. He is writing about the moral injunction 'Thou shalt not kill' and of the way its hold on individuals had declined during the time of the First World War (1950, vol. iv, pp. 311–12):

> When the frenzied conflict of this war shall have been decided, every one of the victorious warriors will joyfully return to his home, his wife and his children, undelayed and undisturbed by any thought of the enemy he has slain. . .It is worthy of note that such primitive races as still inhabit the earth. . .act differently in this respect, or did so act until they came under the influence

of our civilisation. The savage. . .when he returns victorious from the war-path, may not set foot in his village nor touch his wife until he has atoned for the murders committed in war by penances which are often prolonged and toilsome. This may be presumed, of course, to be the outcome of superstition; the savage still goes in fear of the avenging spirits of the slain. But the spirits of the fallen enemy are nothing but the expression of his own conscience, uneasy on account of his blood-guiltiness; behind this superstition lurks a vein of ethical sensitiveness which has been lost by us civilised men.

Freud, contrary to what he was written elsewhere, denies that the penances to which he refers are the outcome of superstition. He does not see the 'fear of the avenging spirits of the slain' as a superstition, but as the expression of genuine moral sentiments and reactions. Contrast this with what he says about Catholic penances in the last passage I quoted. There he was thinking of what is sham. In the case of the savages of Australia and Tierra del Fuego, however, Freud finds the meaning of their beliefs in their practice which he takes at face value, namely as the making of penance. This is not the same thing as the appeasement of one's conscience. What a pity Freud did not remain true to the spirit of the words I have just quoted when he wrote about religion.

5

Love and Morality

1 Acquiring Values and the Formation of Conscience

Freud said (1933, p. 89): 'Conscience is no doubt something within us, but it has not been there from the beginning. . . Small children are notoriously amoral.' It is certainly true that morality is something we acquire from early childhood onwards and that this is a continual process — just as the capacity to think is something we acquire from early childhood onwards. But I don't think that it follows from this that what we learn is to observe rules, conventions, which we would rather not have to observe, because of what we forfeit in doing so. Nor does it follow that we observe them because something in ourselves, conscience, compels us to do so. Thus Jung's remark that 'morality is not imposed from outside: we have it in ourselves from the start'. But here too we have to be careful.

Freud does not speak of values but of conventions conceived of as rules of behaviour. He also speaks of our admiration of people for their qualities of character and also of our idealization of them, by which he means exaggerating the degree to which they have these qualities and minimizing the degree to which they may also have opposite qualities. As he puts it (1950, vol. iv, p. 296): 'A human being is seldom altogether good or bad; he is usually "good" in one relation and "bad" in another, or "good" in certain external circumstances and in others decidely "bad".' He thus regards 'idealization' as a defensive posture provoked by anxiety. On the whole, associating ideals with idealization he does not recognize the way in which they may inspire people and sometimes, by bringing out the best in them, contribute to their development. He sees that admiration and trust have an important role to play in early as well as in later moral development, and 'identification' is the cornerstone of his account of how the child acquires a morality, becomes a moral individual. Before we can appreciate the assets as well as the shortcomings of this account I should like to give a sketch of what, as I see it, acquiring a morality or moral values involves, and how much of this consists of coming to have a conscience.

Acquiring moral values does involve, though it cannot be equated with, coming to have a moral vocabulary and coming to behave in accordance with those values. What is important is coming to have *regard* for these values, and this is a change in the affective life of the individual. This will show in the spirit of his behaviour and actions and in his attitude towards the situations which call for those actions. One of the marks in question is that he will do what he does *willingly*, even when it is difficult and involves facing danger or making sacrifices. Often it will be done as a matter of course, with the agent fully behind what he does. Another mark is that he will see sense in what he does, it will *make sense* to him, whether or not he can articulate this sense. Obviously if it did not make sense he could not do it willingly, nor could he be behind what he does. As he develops he will be able to make more sense of what he does and this will sustain him in his effort to keep faith with his values when this faith is tried. It will also enable him to better discern what claims these values make on him in particular situations. There is no question that we are dealing with the growth of responsibility, which involves being ready to answer for one's actual and projected actions and to take blame for their consequences when things go wrong. We are dealing with the growth of the individual towards autonomy. Freud is right in thinking that this involves greater independence from one's parents, reflected in one's subsequent relationships with other people. But he is wrong to ignore how much the growth of such independence is part of the process of acquiring a morality, part of the continual change in the relation of the individual to his values.

I am sure that our 'moral education' begins almost as soon as we are born, certainly long before we begin to speak. I am not, of course, thinking of anything like the inculcation of values and attitudes, and certainly nothing to which we can attribute a self-conscious aim. That is why I use inverted commas. I am thinking of the building up of a relationship that will be the basis of the child's capacity to form other relationships and the foundation of his capacity to learn — for any kind of learning involves the ability to understand, to observe rules, to obey instructions, to submit willingly to some kind of discipline. Obviously values come later, with language, even if they may not be taught directly at all. But at this earliest stage I am thinking primarily of the building-up of trust between mother and child, and the growth of love. There are already serious obstacles, in the infant's disappointment, anger and impatience, which his mother can help him overcome.

When we come to learn to speak we have already learned something, we have certain ways of responding and the foundations of an individual character. As children we learn to use moral terms and to respond to other people's use of them in conjunction with learning how to behave. We learn, for instance, what to call a 'lie' and also that a lie is something that is normally condemned. We learn not to lie, to refrain from lying when it seems the easy way out, and also to feel ashamed when we do. We learn not only to say 'That is a lie' in appropriate circumstances but also to condemn what we so describe. We thus come to use these words to express our condemnation; and when we confess that we have lied we do so with contrition. At first the connection between our use of the word and what we feel stands isolated. We feel ashamed simply because we have been shamed. But as we learn to use new words and to say new things, the aspect under which we see what a person said or did when we describe it as a lie acquires new dimensions. We see it as breaking someone's trust, for instance, and as showing disregard for him. These new words and the affective attitude which come to be linked with their use give support to our reactions to dishonesty. The isolated connections begin to form a network and this makes it possible for us now to give content to our condemnation of lying.

We learn moral language and acquire moral values in harness. The circumstances in which we learn the language, what we learn it in conjunction with, the situations in which we learn to put it to work, give it a special role in our lives. In this role the aspects which the use of moral terms brings into focus and the sentiments which these aspects evoke in us are internally connected. These are 'connections of meaning' since learning them is part of learning the meaning of the terms in question. But it is possible for a child to learn the use or meaning of these terms without acquiring the values implicit in the language. He may learn what it is to lie and that it is something that is generally condemned, without coming to care for honesty or condemn lying himself.

Still what interests me now is the way in which learning moral language and moral values (i.e. belief in these values) go together and are part of the same training — training not necessarily in any formal sense. This training, in the form of praise and blame, encouragement and reward, rebuke and punishment, takes place in the course of the development of relationships in which the child meets love, anger, sorrow and gratitude, learns to care for, consider and help others, to give up things for them, to co-operate and, in certain cases, to look up to and emulate them. He develops expectations with regard to others and learns to respond to their expectations with regard to him. He learns to make promises and to rely on those made by others, to trust and be trusted. He develops a sense of responsibility and begins to act on his own behalf in the light of conerns which are now his.

Acquiring values, learning standards of behaviour and criticism, is a central part of the formation of a child's identity and character. The child does not learn rules of conduct which are backed by emotions that come to attach themselves to these by reward and rebuke. The emotions are *moral* emotions, and they develop in the course of early personal interactions — love and the desire to be worthy of it, gratitude and guilt, the wish to make amends, the desire of approval. What rules there are make sense in relation to these emotions and desires. Certainly praise and blame, reward and admonishment, play a role in his learning to observe rules of conduct. But the praise and blame that play this role are already endowed with *moral* significance for him. His response cannot be detached from his feelings for those who praise and blame him and for those in whose presence he is praised and rebuked. They are expressions of acceptance and rejection by members of a moral community of which the family is the earliest prototype. They mean that he is worthy or unworthy of those he looks up to. Accordingly he responds with pride and gratitude, or with shame, grief and dejection.

If the child were not responsive to praise and blame, if he were devoid of love and pity, incapable of gratitude, sorrow and shame, I doubt that he would learn any rules of conduct or come to see any moral sense in them. This is the truth to which Jung's words draw attention. Further, unless these sentiments are shared and reciprocated, it is hard to imagine how a people could have moral beliefs. For the child to develop such sentiments there must be situations capable of evoking them. This presupposes forms of thought and appraisal of which he becomes capable through acquiring language and other skills. Since these sentiments and the responses in which they find expression presuppose some intellectual appreciation they are already susceptible of criticism. Thus criticism and reasoning may well have a role to play in early moral teaching. They certainly have an important role to play in later phases of moral development when the individual comes to face situations which test his values or comes into contact with new values that make a bid for his allegiance.

To what extent parents make use of reasoning in the early stages depends on their moral outlook. Some parents will encourage and others will discourage any early search for reasons in their children: 'Why should I share my toys with other children?' 'Why should I not laugh at him when he makes a fool of himself?' 'Why is it naughty to pull the cat's tail?' But the answers given already take much for granted; and if they could not do so the questions themselves would hardly make sense. Perhaps the mother says: 'If someone else did that to you, you would not like it' — hoping to get the child to accept that others are entitled to the consideration he takes for granted for himself. If the lesson he learns is to be more than a prudential one, his mother will try to get him to connect what he is doing to the cat, or a friend of whom he is jealous, with someone doing something similar to someone he cares for: 'If someone did that to your mother, she wouldn't like it. Now *you* wouldn't like that to happen, would you?' Or: 'You wouldn't do that to your mother, would you?' This presupposes that the child is not indifferent to his mother, that he would respond to her pain with sorrow, that he would be dejected if he hurt her, that he is capable of pity. Otherwise his mother's reply to his questions would have no moral force.

So even if we grant, as I do, that reasoning and criticism can play a part in early moral teaching, we must admit that at the bottom of these reasons are the child's primitive affective reactions. It is these that are extended, built on, and modified in the course of his moral development. This is made possible by other forms of learning. As the child learns to participate in new forms of thought and activity the foundation is laid for *new* responses and *new* sentiments. What direction this development will take depends on the forms of thought and activity with which the child comes into contact. What is built up in the earlier part of the child's moral development is thus what makes it possible for him to have a place on which to stand morally. His acquisition of moral beliefs depends on that. It is because he has such a place to stand on that he can question what his parents tell him. Coming to have such a place also means acquiring a certain measure of autonomy and independence. The child no longer merely complies; he sees some sense or point in what he is asked to do and so wants to do it on his own behalf. As he develops, other moral influences begin to impinge on his life, influences which he embraces and is modified by, or criticizes and rejects. These are influences he meets in becoming a member of new groups, in forming new friendships, in coming to be involved in new activities, in entering new movements. He may be critical or uncritical; but where he is critical, it is the place on which he already stands that enables him to weigh and appreciate what he meets.

Thus while there is room for reason in a child's moral learning and development, the possibility of its operation presupposes the existence of something to which the child is not morally indifferent − people for whom he cares, relationships in which there is room for give and take, trust and gratitude, guilt and grief. Coming to a conception of other people is largely possible only in surroundings where the child can form such relationships. So in the beginning is the affective response, shared and reciprocated, which is neither reasonable nor unreasonable − or rather the propensity to its development, except under special conditions which hamper or thwart it.

The point is not merely a temporal one. The possibility of moral judgement presupposes the reality of some moral norm or value. Such values exist independently of whether or not individual people show recognition of their reality. What constitutes this reality is the place they have in the life of a community. The kind of response its members exhibit in particular situations that arise in this life provides the post at which their values are stationed. Someone asks: 'Why is that a reprehensible thing to do?' We may, in response, compare it with other things he finds reprehensible, things about the moral character of which he is in no doubt. There must be such things − acts, motives, persons to the moral character of which he responds without reflection. Alternatively we may give him descriptions of the act which will make clear the moral character we see in it. We may see that it was a reprehensible thing to do because it involved cheating, or letting someone down, or making money out of his distress. Once this is granted there should be no doubt about the original moral claim. But if he doesn't see that cheating is wrong, or that capitalizing on someone's distress is reprehensible, then either his moral beliefs are radically at variance with ours, or his moral development has suffered an early arrest or undergone a decline.

These individual judgements we make in particular cases are interconnected and they give each other mutual support. The fact that we can always refer from one to others in supporting it may disguise their 'ground level' character. But the truth remains that such a judgement is as much a verbal expression of our affective response to the particular situation as the feeling it evokes is an expression of our apprehension. Here expression of affect and apprehension are two sides of the same coin. It is in such 'ground level' judgements that the agreement in our verbal and affective responses interlock — even though they may come apart in individual cases. By 'ground level' I mean that there is nothing more fundamental to which we can appeal to justify them, that the affective reactions of which these judgements are the verbal expression are 'unreasoned'.

To speak as Wittgenstein does, one could say that moral words are connected with the primitive, natural expression of certain feelings. A child, for instance, recoils before a brutal act, and then adults talk to him and teach him exclamations and, later, sentences. They teach the child new moral behaviour (see Wittgenstein, 1963, sec. 244). 'But this is not the *end* of the language-game: it is the beginning' (sec. 290). Pretty early in the course of this development words or sentences like 'Good for you' and 'That was a naughty thing to do' begin to express more than feelings, pro- and con-attitudes. They become a vehicle of apprehension and, as such, contestable. The child can then ask why his parents say that what he did was naughty, and why they praise his little sister for what she did. But he must already have learnt a fair amount before he can ask such questions. What he will have learnt will depend on the kind of activities that go on around him, the language that is used in connection with them, and the ideas that belong to this language.

Where or at what point does conscience come into this? Freud sometimes speaks as if it is conscience which makes us moral, conscience which makes us feel guilty when we do something wrong. But it is because we are moral, i.e. have regard for certain moral values, that we have pangs of conscience when we disregard those values in what we do or omit. Those pangs, the guilt that we feel, are an expression of our regard for moral values. In his book on Freud, Wollheim says that Freud has reversed one of our conventional moral views (1971, p. 197): 'It is not (as we ordinarily think) that we desist from aggression because we have a very rigorous moral ideal but, rather, we have a rigorous moral ideal just because, or to the degree to which, we have renounced aggression.' Let me quote Freud's own words (1949d, p. 79; 1949f, pp. 113–14):

> It is remarkable that the more a man checks his aggressive tendencies towards others the more tyrannical, that is aggressive, he becomes in his ego-ideal. The ordinary view sees the situation the other way around: the standard set up by the ego-ideal seems to be the motive for the suppression of aggressiveness. The fact remains, however, as we stated it.
>
> In the beginning conscience (more correctly, the anxiety which later became conscience) was the cause of instinctual renunication, but later this relation is reversed. Every renunciation then becomes a dynamic fount of conscience; every fresh abandonment of gratification increases its severity and intolerance.

If this is meant to be an account of the formation of conscience, it will not do at all for the reasons I have already suggested. On the other hand, if it is an observation about the conditions under which a man who already has certain moral beliefs becomes morally intolerant, uses the moral failures of others as an excuse to hound and oppress them while feeling righteous, that is a different matter. For what we have there is not the formation or development of conscience, but its distortion.

It is true that such a man's motives for hounding and oppressing others cannot be understood without reference to the values that enter his judgements of them. Nevertheless what he does, the attitudes he takes, the feelings he gives vent to, are not related to these values in the way they are, for instance, in the case of a man who intervenes in an act of injustice, takes the witness stand against the perpetrator, or publicly condemns certain practices. I am assuming that in the latter case he gains nothing and derives no satisfaction. Christians have sometimes spoken of hating the evil such a man does, not the man himself. But if such a distinction is difficult to make, we can describe it as hating the man only for the evil he does and no further. Whereas in the cases Freud had in mind the intolerance is not of evil, but of the man — because he represents something one hates in oneself or enjoys something which one feels prevented from enjoying. Here if one hounds the other person one would be doing two things: denying the disturbing truth that one is like him and indulging in the evil one 'condemns'. One's attitude may well be harsh because one begrudges the concessions one has made to values one does not really care for and is envious of the man who does not make such concessions.

Freud would agree with this account, except in so far as I have not mentioned the role of projection in the way moral hostility is built up in such a case. I speak of 'moral hostility' because what attracts or provokes it is what is seen under a moral aspect, in an unfavourable moral light. But this does not make it into a moral reaction, one that springs from moral concern and can be attributed to conscience. Wicked deeds have often been performed in the name of conscience.

Acts, responses, judgements which can be attributed to conscience are those that are inspired by the subject's concern for moral values in which he believes. If one could speak of the 'motive force' or 'energy' of conscience, in the sense of what inspires or moves a man to action, then this is his concern for these values. Such concern is not, of course, something directed to an abstraction, as Kant pictures it (see Kant, 1959). It is what finds expression in his actions and feelings in particular situations, actions that involve sympathy, loyalty, pity for individual people.

Freud's view that the energy of conscience is 'aggression' cannot, therefore, be correct. Of course, an act of conscience can easily involve anger; but the anger in question is subordinate to love and moral concern, whereas in the cases Freud has in mind this relation is reversed: it is the concern that is subordinated to anger. The person is much more angry with the person he sees as transgressing certain values than concerned about what is thus violated, undermined or damaged. He feels a greater identity, unconsciously, with the man who attracts his anger than with his victim. Thus both Freud and Ernest Jones see that if this is what it means to side with morality one should not be surprised if it brings 'the absence of love in life' (Freud, 1949b, pp. 360–1). Jones is quite clear that this siding with morality 'subserves a defensive or preservative function' (1937, p. 2) and that while many of those who engage in it 'become reliable and decent citizens. . . for their neighbours they present the drawback of being more or less hard-hearted and intolerant people' (p. 3). But, of course, what is in question is not conscience as such but its perversion.

Freud speaks of conscience, or the super-ego as he calls it, as a permanent faculty of the mind. One objection to this is that it ignores the fact that it is only in a restricted class of moral actions and attitudes that we refer to conscience at all. Normally where we respond to the moral features presented by situations that face us, conscience does not come into our actions; nor does it come in when we have to exercise deliberate judgement, to reason about and weigh the matter before us. Where we speak of someone having acted conscientiously or with moral scruples, we do not necessarily mean to refer to the exercise of his conscience. We mean that he acted with care, that in his actions he showed regard for moral values. We speak of conscience where a man pulls back from an action he is tempted to take, where he is troubled by an action in which he succumbs to temptation or gives in to threat, where he feels responsible for someone's suffering, where he feels there is something he can do to alleviate someone else's misfortune. Where such a misfortune provokes him to action, where it stops him minding his own business, we speak of him as 'a man of conscience'. Thus Camus said that 'conscience is born in revolt', that is where one can no longer put up with someone else's oppression, tolerate injustice. But we have seen how open this is to abuse. Again we speak of conscience where a man is persecuted for his moral beliefs: we speak of the 'prisoner of conscience'. But, once more, we have to be clear about the motives of the man who, for instance, sides with the underdog. As Simone Weil has pointed out, to side with him from pure compassion is a very rare thing. If so, let us be careful not to speak of conscience where a man acts out of a grudge against those he sees as oppressor, one who thrives on the conspiratorial relationships he forms with those who take a stand against 'the oppressor'. What moves him is not love, but hatred; not regard for the oppressed, but concern for what Kant called 'the dear self' (1959, p. 28).

2 *Conscience and the Super-ego*

Freud's interest in men's motives and 'the vicissitudes of the instincts' fixed his attention on just such cases and led him to identify conscience with its perverted varieties. He wrote about both the formation of conscience in its early beginnings and the troubles which an over-strict conscience can bring into a man's life. But he only managed to focus on the *tyranny* of a conscience that has become lopsided or perverted. What such a conscience demands is its own satisfaction, and a man so tyrannized will do the right thing not because it is right but in order to appease his conscience. Thus Freud speaks of the ego having to 'serve three harsh masters', 'three tyrants', one of these being the super-ego (1933, p. 108; 1949d, pp. 82–3). His view that men need a reason, a motive, in order to act morally goes with that. The reason at first is to keep the love of their parents, which they dread losing. This is later transformed into the motive of avoiding a 'bad conscience', which is equally painful (1949f, pp. 106–7; 1950b, vol. iv, p. 297).

What is the truth behind this view? While Freud uses the terms 'conscience' and 'super-ego' interchangeably, he thinks of the super-ego as the precursor of conscience. According to Freud the super-ego takes its final form at the time when the child is struggling to resolve inner conflicts centring around the Oedipus complex. Freud stresses the role of identification in its formation – especially identification with the parent of the same sex; the father in the case of the boy. What leads to this identification? Freud mentions the rivalry which the boy feels with his father over his mother's love and his fear of 'punishment'. I put 'punishment' in inverted commas, for it is largely the expectation of hostile, even savage, treatment on account of his own hostile feelings. What is in question is an expectation of retaliation derived from his own primitive impulse to retaliate when subjected to interference and hostility. Freud sees identification as a means of averting this threat: 'If you cannot beat the father, then you may as well join him.' He sees it as a way of partaking of the father's strength. He also sees it, more positively, as a way of 'keeping' his father, in so far as he loves the father, at a time when he is acquiring some independence. I say 'positively' in the sense that in this respect it does not serve a defensive purpose, but is itself the form taken by the 'resolution' of the Oedipus complex.

Through identification the boy thus takes on aspects of his father's character; he takes over some of his father's demands and expectations, and also some of his ways of thinking and moral beliefs. In so far as the balance in the boy's feelings for his father is tipped on the side of hostility, the identification with him will be largely defensive and the super-ego will be characterized largely by reaction-formation. Freud's view is that while this is a matter of degree, the child is always somewhat ambivalent in his feelings towards his parents and hostility therefore inevitably plays some part in the formation of the super-ego.

It is worth noting that this is a more moderate view from the one that claims that the super-ego derives its force from aggressiveness. Here Freud is approaching the question of the nature and formation of conscience from the side of the child's relationships with his parents, where he sees the role of both love and hate, fear as well as confidence. Whereas in developing the more extreme view he approaches the question from the side of considerations of the place of morality in human life, and his philosophical preconceptions colour the view he develops.

What are the positive features emphasized in his more moderate view, neglected in his extreme statements? They are the place accorded to the way children take on their parents' characteristics, including the way they feel and think about things, through identification, and the role which love plays in this. What is involved is more than mere copying or imitation; it is a partaking of someone else's fears and expectations, joys and apprehensions by making oneself one with him. The behaviour and responses, gestures and mimicry are then not the result of imitation; they are the spontaneous expressions of what has thus been assimilated. Identification, as Freud points out, is a form of relationship; and the assimilation in question is part of the sharing that dominates such a relationship. There is certainly room for it in the account I have sketched in the previous section. It does play a positive role in the process through which the child acquires new attitudes, and it provides him with the support needed to overcome obstacles to the development of regard for the values he learns from his parents. Certainly identification involves more than what Freud describes in chapter 7 of *Civilization and its Discontents*, namely the internalisation of external compulsion.

Even then, however, there is more to moral learning than identification, for identification does not in itself create genuine autonomy. The actions and responses that have their source in identification with another person are indeed different from those that are motivated by a desire to please or to appease him; but they are still enacted in his shadow. Secondly, acquiring moral values involves more than the taking over of moral attitudes. The affective change which constitutes coming to have regard for these values goes beyond the changes that go with identification. Although I concede that identification does involve the taking over of another person's ways of thinking about things, this still falls short of the growth of understanding that is equally necessary to moral autonomy. It is the values he acquires that beget new responses in the child; and this is more than taking over these responses from the parent with whom the child identifies himself. Acquiring these values, we have seen, involves learning to speak, coming to possess a vocabulary, and so modes of sizing up situations, weighing consequences, criticizing ways of acting. The child develops new sentiments and learns new forms of response in harness with all this. Concentrating exclusively on his identification with his parents does not do justice to this many-sided process of learning

I asked for the truth behind Freud's view of the nature and formation of conscience and I mentioned the place he gives to identification in the development of conscience. I also distinguished between conscience and the super-ego. The super-ego stands to conscience in somewhat the same way in which phantasy stands to reason. Just as reason cannot develop out of what I called 'phantasy thinking', so equally conscience and the kind of criticism which constitutes its exercise cannot develop out of the super-ego. For all this the super-ego represents a quasi-moral mentality which exercises an influence on our conscience, distorting and perverting its criticism. This I believe to be another part of the truth behind Freud's view of the nature of conscience – his view of the super-ego as a tyrannical faculty of the mind. Freud's description of its formation is inadequate as a description of the growth of morality in the child; but it is a description of what really does go on and how in part of his mind the young child does take and react to parental discipline.

In 'The Genesis of the Super-ego' Ernest Jones recognizes this distinction (1955, p. 40): 'The super-ego has several conscious derivations, for instance, conscience, ego-ideal, etc., but it itself has to be carefully distinguished from them.' Other psycho-analysts have also made a distinction here. I am thinking of Erich Fromm and Roger Money-Kyrle who have both characterized Freud's super-ego as an 'authoritarian conscience' in contrast with what they call a 'humanitarian conscience'. It is clear from Fromm's descriptions in *Man for Himself* that what he calls an 'authoritarian conscience' is the 'conscience' of a man who is only externally related to the values which enter his judgements and actions (See Fromm, 1950, chapter 4, section 2a). Fromm does not use the terms 'internal' and 'external' as I am using them. For him the claims of an authority are external until one sides with them; when one does so and oneself comes to support them he describes these as having become internal. This is 'the great change' which Freud speaks of in *Civilisation and its Discontents*. While these claims are external, in Fromm's sense, people act out of fear of punishment and the hope of reward. Yet a man who acts in this way is different from one who has an authoritarian conscience in that the latter has changed sides. This, however, does not make him different in other essential respects (Fromm, 1950, pp. 144–5): 'The most important point of similarity is the fact that the prescriptions of authoritarian conscience are not determined by one's own value judgments but exclusively by the fact that its commands and taboos are pronounced by authorities.' That is, it is not the values in question that matter to him, what he sees in them, but the support of the authority with which he sides or identifies himself. What counts for him is the strength he derives from participating in the strength of the authority who supports them (p. 146). This is what I mean when I say that he is related to these values only 'externally'.

Fromm describes 'humanistic conscience' as a person's 'own voice' as opposed to 'the internalised voice of an authority' (p. 158). But he imagines that the values which give the person's 'own voice' its particular point of view are somehow given by what constitutes the development of the individual's potentials: 'Conscience...is the voice of our true selves which summons us back to ourselves, to live productively, to develop fully and harmoniously — that is, to become what we potentially are' (p. 159). But what are we supposed to be potentially? Here Fromm sneaks in his own values and pretends they are backed by nature. This is a conjuring trick familiar in ethics, but I am not concerned to examine the particular form it takes in Fromm's positive views.

In 'Psycho-analysis and Ethics' Money-Kyrle uses the same words, 'authoritarian' and 'humanistic' conscience, but the distinction he makes derives from Melanie Klein's work, especially her findings regarding the earliest stages of individual development (Money-Kyrle, 1955). These terms are meant to characterize two different kinds of allegiance demanded by different values. By an 'authoritarian morality' Money-Kyrle means a morality which demands obedience, and by a 'humanistic morality' he means one that is based on love — a love of human beings. Obedience is more concerned with a man's actions than with the spirit in which he does them. It is something that can be extracted by force, supported by what produces fear. Punishment is the pain which is meant to ensure that people keep to the right path by reminding them of what will happen if they don't do so. Love, on the other hand, is not something that can be prescribed; it can at best be inspired by ideals. It can also be liberated when it is present in the individual though not accessible to his will. Money-Kyrle argues that psycho-analysis can help here. As for punishment, it can be more than a way of ensuring that people obey certain precepts. It can be the form under which a spiritual awakening takes place in someone who has offended against certain values (see Dilman, 1976).

Following Melanie Klein, Money-Kyrle finds the prototype

of such awakening in the life of the infant when he is first overcome with dismay upon realizing that the mother with whom he has been enraged and whom he has destroyed in his phantasies is the same person whom he loves dearly. This is what Melanie Klein terms the 'depressive position' because it involves experiencing feelings of a depressive character, guilt and dismay, of which being sorry is a later and more sophisticated variety. Melanie Klein would say that being sorry is not something that the child is taught, although saying 'I am sorry' is. It is a natural, primitive reaction in someone who has spoiled, hurt or done harm to something or someone that is dear to him. She would say that the mother's role as 'educator' is not to teach it but to create conditions favourable to its development — or at least to avoid conditions that would hamper it.

Thus Money-Kyrle distinguishes between 'persecutory' and 'depressive' guilt — guilt based on fear and guilt based on love. The former is the prerogative of an 'authoritarian' conscience. In the earliest stages of infancy the expectation of harsh treatment is the expectation of retaliation for the bad feelings, the savage phantasies, which are provoked in the child by frustration, hunger and discomfort. It is not necessarily based on the experience of actual parental treatment. This fear of retaliation in the infant for his bad feelings is the earliest prototype of guilt and is the precursor of the super-ego which Freud described as 'the heir of the Oedipus complex'. As Money-Kyrle puts it (1955, p. 431), in Melanie Klein's view 'the super-ego, which Freud discovered, does not begin, as he believed, about the age of five, but is already at that age approaching its final form after five years of previous development.' But it is not this that is really new in Melanie Klein's contribution. What is new is her introduction of a different form of guilt into the child's early affective life and relationships, one neglected by Freud — depressive guilt and restitutive or reparative responses. As another Kleinian analyst, Marion Milner, puts it (1977, p. 67):

> It was surely clear, to me at least, that one needed no imposed moral code to teach one that it was bad to spoil what one loved, good to preserve and keep it safe. Thus it did certainly seem that there is an inherent as well as an implanted morality. It did

certainly seem that one struggles to control greediness and aggression in oneself, not only through fear of being punished or losing other people's love and respect, but also to avoid injuring or even destroying whatever seems to oneself to be beautiful and lovable.

What she is calling attention to is not so much an 'inherent morality' as primitive moral reactions which may be built on and extended in the child's later contacts with different forms of morality. These are the reactions which may equally be stifled in the course of his later development. These reactions of grief, dismay, depressive guilt are, as we have already seen, expressions of love (see chapter 3, section 2 above). They presuppose that something is dear to their subject, so dear that doing it harm or seeing it hurt is painful.

Experiences that undermine the child's confidence in himself and trust in others, those that increase fear and anxiety in him, those that provoke rage and anger, will stifle the development of these responses, diminish his capacity to feel depressive guilt. The ground will thus be prepared for the formation of the kind of conscience Freud calls the super-ego — covering the 'authoritarian' conscience dominated by 'persecutory guilt', the over-conscientiousness of the obsessive neurotic dominated by 'reaction-formations', and the hypo-paranoid conscience characterized by extreme self-righteousness and censoriousness. The conflict between the ego and the super-ego is sharpest in cases of melancholia and absent in cases of mania where 'the ego and the ego-ideal have fused together' (Freud, 1949c, p. 107).

Very different experiences favour the development of a genuine conscience, experiences which help the child's capacity to love and trust others. Only these will make him willing to put himself out for others, to risk danger for their sake, to feel for them in their suffering, to take their side when they are hounded or treated unjustly, to resist exploiting them when in a position to gain from their weakness, to feel guilty when he hurts or harms them, to wish to make restitution. It is these that we regard as expressions of conscience. The tendencies — aggressive and destructive — which go into the building up of the super-ego are actually reduced, as Melanie Klein points out, by experiences which promote love and trust. For seeing the reflection of friendly qualities in other people 'reduces persecutory anxiety' (Klein, 1952, p. 208). The ability to make reparation decreases depression. Thus she speaks of the 'progressive assimilation of the super-ego by the ego' (p. 214).

Where such an assimilation has not taken place in the course of a person's development, psycho-analysis can help, as Freud points out, to reduce the tyranny of the super-ego. But Freud does not shed much light on how this happens. Melanie Klein does. It involves the reduction of what may be called 'secondary' fear and anger, and the 'working through' of guilt and depression as the person is able to make up for the hurtful tendencies that emanate from him. For instance, he may come to be able to say 'I am sorry' and 'Thank you' with greater readiness and not in a placatory way, to say these things and mean them. When these words come from fear or anxiety they are the expression of defensive postures; but the love or concern from which they may come is antithetical to self-defense. It is central to both Freud's and Melanie Klein's thinking that resorting to defensive measures locks an individual's development in a vicious circle.

Once the hold of this circle has been loosened by psycho-analysis the rest can come from the individual. This involves waiting and not running away, enduring anxiety, grief, guilt and depression. This is very different from wallowing in misery, trying to make capital of it, for that too is an evasion, an attempt to reduce the pain by turning it into an advantage. This process of 'working through' is what I am inclined to describe as the integration of the love that the person has into the will. Freud spoke of this as the replacement of repression with self-mastery, but he thought of it too much as the control of the emotions by reason, conceived of as a form of rational self-interest. Melanie Klein put the emphasis on love and this made a radical difference to the psycho-analytic conception of morality and the individual's relation to it (Segal, 1964, p. 61): 'This new capacity to feel concern for his objects helps him (the infant) to learn gradually to control his impulses.' It is interesting to notice that Winnicott calls Melanie Klein's 'depressive position' 'the stage of concern'.

In the first chapter I mentioned Ian Robinson's criticism of a 'modern' attitude towards guilt: 'The removal of the possibility of guilt is the removal of the possibility of significance'. We see now that this possibility of significance is bound up with the possibility of concern. The values that provide the framework within which this concern develops come to the individual from outside, from the life of the society to which they belong. I have stressed how much they have the power to beget new responses and sentiments in the individual. Nevertheless it is equally true, and this is what analysts like Melanie Klein, Marion Milner, Money-Kyrle and others, including Jung, have stressed, that the root of this concern or love lies within the individual and manifests itself in very early reactions to other people, notably the mother. These reactions appear quite spontaneously in the early development of the individual and do not have to be taught: 'The healthy child has a personal sense of guilt, and need not be taught to be guilty or concerned' (Winnicott).

What the 'modern' attitude confuses in its opposition to guilt is 'persecutory' and 'depressive' guilt, and the reduction or removal of the former would neither constitute the removal of 'the possibility of significance', nor would it promote 'licence'. Melanie Klein herself considers this question (1948, p. 72): 'It might be asked, would not too great a reduction of the severity of the super-ego. . .have the opposite result and lead to the abolition of social and ethical sentiments in the child?' Her answer is NO (p. 73): 'In mitigating the severity of the super-ego by lessening the operation of its sadistic constituents that arise from the earliest stages of development. . .analysis prepares the way not only for the achievement of social adaptability in the child, but for the development of moral and ethical standards in the adult.' In this way the super-ego 'gradually becomes transformed into conscience in the true sense of the word' (p. 68). This is also the answer provided by Money-Kyrle when he asks how 'the depressive element in guilt is affected by a deep analysis': 'Analysis, while diminishing the conflicts that lead to depression, increases rather than diminishes the capacity to feel guilt of a depressive kind whenever a "good" object is in any way injured or betrayed' (Money-Kyrle, 1955, p. 434). Ernest

Jones puts this by saying that the removal of a 'substitutive' morality makes way for the growth of a more genuine moral attitude which he calls an 'attitude of love' (see Jones, 1937; Dilman, forthcoming, chapter 11).

It is clear that the psycho-analyst is not concerned with the moral education of his patient and works by loosening or removing his defensive measures, or *per via di levare* as Freud puts it in terms of a metaphor he borrowed from Leonardo da Vinci (see Freud, 1950, vol. i, pp. 253—4). It thus provides him with an opportunity he has missed in earlier life. The removal of defensive attitudes also allows him to give himself to activities going on around him in a way he has not done before and to have deeper contact with people, to respond to their attitudes and learn from them. This would include coming into contact with new values and seeing new sense in old ones, renewing his relationships to them. Thus what had become static will start moving again, moving independently of the analysis. What values he will find and what values will attract him will depend on his external circumstances as well as on what he is like; on who his parents were and what friends he makes, what his profession and interests are and what circles he moves in. But, whatever these values and moral attitudes are, if he is to be genuinely moral in their light he must be himself. The role of analysis here is to free him from, strengthen him against, pressures that would deflect him from being himself. It is in this way that psycho-analysis makes the patient accessible to moral influences, both from within and outside; but it does not provide any such influence itself, except in so far as the analyst shows concern for the patient and demands complete honesty from him.

3 *Authority and Repression*

Freud's negative characterizations have given the impression that he was an enemy of morality. But he had a very high regard for honesty. In fact the workings of psycho-analysis are founded on such regard. What Freud was opposed to is humbug, especially the kind perpetuated in the name of morality. He was against the oppressive use of morality, a morality imposed on people and backed up by coercion. He did not see much virtue in compliance and submissiveness. It is these that he characterized as reaction-formations against the defiance engendered by forcing people to tow the line. So he spoke of 'the severity of the demands by which moral convention oppresses the individual' (Freud, 1949b, p. 361). His talk of 'convention' here is not simply a symptom of philosophical confusion, for morality is indeed little more than a convention if nothing in the individual rises up to meet it. Things get even worse when the individual sides with those who use morality to oppress him, thus himself using morality to keep himself in line and to oppress others, so that the system of oppression is perpetuated (Freud, 1933, p. 95):

> In general, parents and similar authorities follow the dictates of their own super-egos in the upbringing of children. . .They have forgotten the difficulties of their own childhood, and are glad to be able to identify themselves fully at last with their own parents, who in their day subjected them to such severe restraints. The result is that the super-ego of the child is not really built up on the model of the parents, but on that of the parents' super-ego.

It is not authority as such, parental authority, that Freud views with some scepticism, but an authority that is arbitrary, selfish and tyrannical. A parent is being arbitrary when he tells his child to do or not to do something simply because he wishes it: 'Why should I do it?' 'Because I tell you so.' He is arbitrary when he is not consistent: one day he forbids the child to do something to which on another day he has no objection. He is selfish in that he does not have the child's interest at heart, or is incapable of visualizing it. The exercise of benevolent authority, in other words caring for the child, takes love and imagination. A parent is tyrannical, seeks to impose his will on the child, because he is sadistic, selfish, or very anxious. He cannot tolerate any naughtiness or spontaneity in the child; the discipline he imposes is a way of controlling his own anxiety. Whether the child reacts to this regime or not, whether he becomes compliant or rebellious, he will inherit these anxieties, they will be passed onto him.

I said earlier that what Fromm and Money-Kyrle call an 'authoritarian morality' is one in which obedience is the central notion. This notion has a role to play in every morality, even if the importance attached to obedience varies with the kind of morality. What Fromm and Money-Kyrle have in mind is an obedience based on fear rather than one that springs from willing consent. Such consent is based on regard. One can, of course, have regard for force and consent to be its instrument. Here the person in question would *not* be siding with authority out of fear and weakness, and his conscience would not be false, born out of a defensive posture. Yet it would not be one built on love of human beings. On the contrary, such a person would consider any stirrings of love or tenderness in himself as an expression of weakness to be mastered or overcome. I do not know what psychoanalysis has to say about the formation of such a Nietzschean conscience, which I distinguish from the Freudian super-ego — although Erich Fromm does not — except that it is modelled on the conscience of parents which bears this character.

Let us return to my original point, that Freud is not sceptical about authority as such, but about a special kind of authority which relies on the fear it inspires to bring about submission and compliance. Not all authority is of this kind. I have characterized the exercise of benevolent authority as caring. I am sure that Freud would have agreed that just as the child needs some physical support in learning to walk, so he needs the support of parental authority in learning self-discipline. Purely philosophical considerations show that if he is to achieve autonomy he must have a will to exercise, and that such a will is acquired in the first place in learning to respond to commands. But I am thinking of something that goes beyond this. For the conditions presupposed by the possibility of acquiring the capacity for intentional action are relevant to the achievement of autonomy and the formation of a servile character alike. This is so because in order to become servile or submissive a person must have a will he can surrender to a tyrannical authority. I am thinking of the way a benevolent authority provides a framework for the child's spontaneity. Without such a framework spontaneity would turn into a muddle; it could hardly have a direction. It should, therefore, be distinguished from the curtailment of the child's spontaneity.

The child would not only be confused if no one told him how far he could go, he would also be frightened. If he were left entirely to his own devices he would be swamped by feelings that would not be conducive to his growth. If his parents indulge him out of weakness, for instance, he will not later be able to stand up for himself. If he can manipulate them and always succeed in getting his own way, he will not grow to have respect for them or regard for anybody else. This will leave his life pretty empty. As Harry and Bonaro Overstreet put it (1954, pp. 59—60): 'It is hard for a child to win through to a healthy self-acceptance. . .if he is so pampered and indulged that he has no chance to learn the stimulating resistances of the world's problems and materials — and therefore no chance either to assimilate disappointment or to feel pride in accomplishment.'

My point is that the antithesis of the kind of authority which Freud regards as harmful to the development of the child is not lack of authority, if that means indulging the child, spoiling him, never saying 'no' to him. In *The Future of an Illusion*, speaking about the instinctual renunciations demanded by culture, Freud writes (1949e, p. 25):

> If one imagined its prohibitions removed, then one could choose any woman who took one's fancy as one's sexual object, one could kill without hesitation one's rival or whoever interfered with one in any other way, and one could seize what one wanted of another man's goods without asking his leave: how splendid, what a succession of delights, life would be!

This comes from what is shallow and superficial in Freud. I think it would be a mistake to bring down his contribution to the level of this passage and others like it in Freud's writings.

6

Human Nature and Culture

1 'Man as essentially Self-seeking and Pleasure-loving'

There are two distinctions in Freud's thinking which should
not be confused, the second of which will concern us in this
chapter. One is the distinction between appearance and reality
in a particular person's life. The idea is that he may be different in many ways from the way he appears to himself. He
may be deceived about himself and, indeed, seek to deceive
himself. Hence the idea of how things stand in his unconscious
mind, the unconscious particular to this individual. Secondly,
Freud wishes to distinguish between the apparent variety in
the behaviour, attitudes and ideals we find among men and the
real springs of these with respect to which, at bottom, all men
are essentially alike. Thus he speaks of the instinctual endowment with which each man begins his life. This is the respect in
which men transcend the culture of the particular society in
which they grow up, the respect in which they belong to
nature, the respect in which they remain relatively unmodified
despite their interaction with the culture of their society.
Freud's concept of an impersonal id is meant to bring this
into prominence. I think that in this idea of human nature
truth and confusion are inextricably mixed. I hope to try
and disentangle them in this chapter.

In *Civilization and its Discontents* he speaks of men as
originally and unalterably aggressive and self-seeking (1949f,
pp. 85—6):

> Men are not gentle, friendly creatures wishing to love, who simply
> defend themselves if they are attacked, but. . .a powerful measure
> of desire for aggression has to be reckoned as part of their instinc-
> tual endowment. . .This aggressive cruelty usually lies in wait for

some provocation, or else it steps into the service of some other purpose, the aim of which might as well have been achieved by milder measures. In circumstances that favour it, when those forces in the mind which ordinarily inhibit it cease to operate, it also manifests itself spontaneously and reveals men as savage beasts to whom the thought of sparing their own kind is alien.

He goes on to support this claim by a review of history — the early migrations, the Huns, the Mongols, the sack of Jerusalem by the pious Crusaders, the horrors of the First World War. 'Civilised society is perpetually menaced with disintegration through this primary hostility of men towards one another.' (p. 86). He regards men's interest in their common work as not sufficient to hold them together. He thinks of the high moral ideals which men adopt as cultural artifices which have the aim of regulating men's behaviour towards one another and holding their greed and aggression in check. Nevertheless, he believes, they remain 'completely at variance with original human nature'. However civilized and moral men may become, they remain at bottom selfish and aggressive. Their consideration and love for one another does not go deep and cannot be an expression of what they really are like. Love being sexual in character aims at pleasure and, as such, is self-seeking.[1]

Here Freud is not merely reminding us of what men are *capable* of, even the best of men, which it would be sentimental to ignore. Nor is he simply drawing attention to the difficulties of achieving high moral standards and remaining true to one's moral beliefs. He is telling us what men are *actually* like — unalterably and inevitably. But in what sense 'inevitable' and why 'unalterably'? The answer to these questions brings in certain *a priori* assumptions about human action and the individual's relation to society. These need criticism and have been criticized. Their criticism constitutes a critique of Freud's 'hedonism'.

Behind Freud's view that men are at bottom self-seeking there is some pull towards the idea that this cannot be otherwise. This pull emanates from confusions that centre around the idea that whatever a man does he must be doing what he wants. Whether he conforms to other people's wishes because

[1] This idea was examined and criticized in chapters 1 and 3 above.

he is afraid to displease them, does something to please some-one he loves, or helps someone for whom he feels sorry, he does what he himself wants. He may be doing what someone else wants, but only because he wants to do it. Hence in all these cases he acts to satisfy himself.

There are many confusions here. To begin with the case where a man acts out of fear or anxiety: this is very different from the case where he acts out of concern for another person, whether out of love or pity. In the former case, whether he is afraid for himself or for someone else, he is not doing what he wants. For were it not for the threat or danger that he fears, he would not do what he does. If, in a different case, he does what he does to appease or placate someone, then he is indeed thinking of himself. But then he is not doing what he wants: his anxiety prevents him from considering what that may be. If, on the other hand, he does something to please someone he loves then he would be doing what he wants, and he may find pleasure in doing so. But this is not to say that pleasure or satisfaction is the object of his actions, that his actions are self-seeking. In other words, it is not true that a man always does what he wants. Nor is it true that where he does what he wants he is acting selfishly or seeking his own satisfaction. What he does may be what *he* wants to do, but this does not mean that he does what he does for *himself*. To think so is to assimilate an action done to please someone to one done to appease him. It is not a necessary truth that a man does what he wants. The fact that he has a reason or motive for doing it does not imply that he is doing what he wants. Nor is it a necessary truth that a man who does what he wants pursues his own pleasure or interest. Both ideas are symptoms of confusion.

It is true that where a man does what he wants he will find some fulfilment in what he does. Where he neglects to do what he wants, where anxieties and considerations of gain deflect him from asking himself what he wants to do, the possibility of happiness will elude him. But this does not mean that man seeks his own happiness, that he is concerned to maximize his happiness or minimize his unhappiness. Freud asks 'what the behaviour of men reveals as to the purpose and object of their lives' and answers that men 'seek

happiness, they want to become happy and remain so'
(1949f, pp. 26—7). Further down he says (pp. 57—8) that
'the force behind all human activities is a striving towards the
two convergent aims of profit and pleasure'. Here we have
Freud's 'pleasure principle' which he claimed reigns supreme
in the unconscious or the id. This belongs to his so-called
'metapsychology'. At the level of clinical experience it is
mirrored in his emphasis on defensive measures in people's
mental make-up. He saw them as trying to keep anxiety at
bay and this preoccupation as colouring many of their
activities. But then this is something from which psycho-
analysis aims to relieve people and so cannot regard it as
inevitable.

Why, then, was Freud inclined to do so in his more specula-
tive moments? Part of the confusion here overlaps with the
one on which I have just commented: A man would not seek
what he seeks if he were adverse to it; if he seeks something
he must want it. But in the sense in which this is a truism it
does not say anything about *what* men want or seek. Yet
there is some temptation to identify it with pleasure or happiness. The only truth I can see here is that, other things being
equal, everyone wants to be happy — at least, no one would
be unhappy from choice. But this little phrase 'other things
being equal' is meant to exclude a variety of situations which
one is apt to forget. Men are willing to put up with suffering
and unhappiness for what they believe and for the people
they love. Engrossed in activities to which they have given
themselves, they may care little about the dangers and dis-
comforts to which these activities may expose them. The fact
that they are behind their actions, the fact that they put up
with pain and discomfort willingly, does not mean that
they do so for the sake of some reward in which they will
find happiness, as Freud's 'reality principle' implies. In the
above qualified sense, to say that men want to be happy
does not mean that men *seek* happiness; it does not mean
that they pursue the activities in which they engage as a means
to the further and ultimate end of happiness.

So we need to be clear about the relation of men's 'desire
for happiness' to the variety of things they want and activities
they pursue. To say that 'men want to be happy' is one thing,

to say that they want the different things they seek as a means to happiness is quite another thing. In fact, happiness is something that always eludes those who seek it directly. Understandably, since it has no substance of its own. One man may find happiness in pursuing his interests, another in devotion to his family, a third in the company of friends. Freud recognizes this but goes wrong in thinking that men pursue the different things in which they find happiness as a *means* to it (1949f, p. 40): 'There is no sovereign recipe in this matter which suits all; each one must find out for himself by which particular means he may achieve felicity.' But happiness is not something over and above the different things in which men find it. The moment any one of them is made into a means to happiness, it can no longer bring happiness.

There are genuine conceptual links between 'happiness', 'doing what one wants' and 'enjoying what one does'. But doing what one wants does not mean grabbing things for oneself or seeking one's satisfaction. Satisfaction is not the 'object' of one's desires, in the sense of what one seeks, even though when one attains that object one necessarily obtains some satisfaction, namely the satisfaction of one's desire. This is not the same thing as self-satisfaction. The phrase 'doing what one wants' covers a wide variety of things, among them pursuing one's interests, acting in accordance with one's conscience. Equally, we mean to oppose it to a variety of things: doing things for the sake of appearances, because one feels forced to do them, in order to avoid feared consequences. In the face of actions of the latter kind a man cannot find happiness, for such actions if they are widespread in a man's life would desiccate it of any sense.

Again, if someone said that a man who finds no pleasure in anything cannot be happy, he would be making a conceptual point, not advocating a life of pleasure. His point would be that a person who does what he is genuinely interested in will enjoy what he is doing and be enriched by it. It will not be a chore. It is the absence of enjoyment in *this* sense that is incompatible with happiness. Again, the enjoyment one finds in doing what one wants, in pursuing one's interests, is not something over and above the activities in question. Since it does not exist independently of these activities it cannot be obtained in any other way, and it cannot therefore be pursued as an end. What can be so pursued is something different: pleasurable sensations or a good time — except that these things soon become something boring, even if they may still be pursued out of desperation. Simone Weil has pointed out that a life of pleasure is generally pursued to fill a spiritual void, although it can never do so. The British psycho-analyst Fairbairn, who has criticized the hedonism in Freud's theoretical thinking, has pointed out that 'explicit pleasure-seeking represents a deterioration of behaviour' (1952, p. 139). As he puts it further down (p. 157): 'It is only insofar as conditions of adaptation become too difficult for the child that the reality-principle gives place to the pleasure-principle as a secondary and deteriorative (as against regressive) principle of behaviour calculated to relieve tension and provide compensatory satisfaction.' Fairbairn's point is that the pursuit of pleasure is a symptom of the breakdown of a person's capacity to give and take, or the lack of it.

2 'The Duality of Man's Nature'

From the beginning Freud was impressed by the part which inner conflict plays in mental life. This goes back to his early disagreement with Breuer over the mechanism of hysteria: 'He preferred a still quasi-physiological theory. . .I understood the psychic cleavage itself as the result of a process of repulsion which I called then defense, later "repression".'[2] Conflict, ambivalence, defence, repression — these are clinical notions. The different emotions and desires, loyalties and identifications that divide a person vary from case to case. Freud was not content to leave it there. He wanted to represent the different divisions and splits within men as modes of an ultimate duality in man's nature and in human life itself. He thought of the particular conflicts, detected by clinical observation, in terms of opposite poles or polarities with reference to which they could be plotted. Hence his dualistic instinct theories. In this way he attempted to give what is observed in the individual a foundation in human nature.

[2] Quoted by Hans Sachs in Sachs, 1945, p. 133. See also Freud, 1948, p. 40.

Hans Sachs sees this dualism as one of the pivots around which Freud's thinking revolved (Sachs, 1945, pp. 33—4):

> This centre in Freud's thoughts, toward which every road and bypath turned, was the dualistic concept — first of the mind, then of life, and ultimately of the Universe. . .He saw everywhere around him the struggle of two opposing forces and used this as a key to the solution of a number of puzzling problems. . .The inner history of the development of psycho-analytic theory is the story of the broadening and deepening of this dualistic-dynamic concept.

One can, quite naturally, regard this dualistic conception as a conception of what man is ultimately like. We shall consider later whether it makes sense to talk of what man is like irrespective of the historical and cultural conditions in which men become individuals. But there is another way of looking at this dualistic conception. One can see Freud as emphasizing actual forces in human life which oppose one another, and considering the phenomena he studies in the light of their conflict or opposition. As such one can see a certain formal similarity between this attempt in Freud and the way some great literary and religious writers have tried to understand men's plight and moral problems in terms of the struggle between good and evil within their souls. One problem here is whether one can speak of the same forces appearing in different forms in dissimilar social conditions. The forces in question are love and hunger or self-preservation, and later love and hate. Love here is to be understood as what finds expression in human life in the form of givingness, creativeness, gratitude, pity, etc., as discussed in chapter 3. By hunger is meant what stands for all expressions of going after what one wants for oneself, protecting and defending it, and by hate what stands for all forms of adversity towards others who stand in one's way, who possess what one would like to have, who thwart one or make one feel the limitation of one's powers.

I call them 'forces' to mean that in them we have what *moves* human beings. Freud speaks of them as 'instincts' — sex and ego instincts, and later life and death instincts. The idea is that love makes for life and growth, in the sense that human beings find life in co-operation and give-and-take with others, that all learning presupposes this form of relatedness, whereas in hate, destructiveness, envy and suspicion, all life and growth is stifled. Yet by calling them 'instincts' Freud assimilates them to biological facts and suggests that they exist independently of the kind of life which makes men what they are — human beings, persons. This does damage to his insight. He ought to have recognized that what transcends particular cultures need not be something that exists independently of the kind of life we find among human beings. I shall develop this point in the final section of this chapter.

I now turn to the members of the pair in Freud's later 'instinct theory' — life and death instincts. I have commented on the former under the title of 'love', so I shall confine myself to the latter under the aspect of 'destructiveness'. It was Freud's later view that this is primarily directed against what the person himself draws sustenance from, and so he referred to it as the death instinct. His idea is that it represents a movement within the soul which seeks the person's own death, physical and spiritual. It may find expression in an ill person's unwillingness to get better, in a withdrawal from contact with other people, and ultimately in suicide. His earlier view was that this is a secondary phenomenon, aggressiveness turned inwards — hence his treatment of sadism and masochism in the *Three Essays*, where he considered it as a phenomenon belonging to sexuality rather than an independent force in human life.

The general question of whether destructive anger and hatred are expressions of destructiveness turned outwards or self-destructiveness is anger and hatred turned inwards is one which I do not readily know what to make of. Clinically both phenomena exist: the turning in of anger and the turning out of self-hatred. Why then consider one as fundamental and the other as a derivative or secondary phenomenon? It may be that doing so is an aspect of Freud's 'essentialism'. Putting this question aside, it seems to me that alongside his idea of love as a force for growth and co-operation in human life, Freud considers that there is a force which counteracts the former's workings — something that divides men, that turns them against each other. I, personally, see a certain continuity between the second pair in each of Freud's two theories of instincts, between ego-instincts and destructiveness, although *prima facie* they seem the opposite of each other, especially if we take the latter as 'self-destructiveness'.

For what are the clinical manifestations of the ego-instincts? Self-defence, including all those 'defensive' phenomena known to psycho-analysis, and the pursuit of the needs of the self. In them we have a movement of the soul in which the person is interested in *taking, keeping* and *preserving* what belongs to him. Clinically, has not psycho-analysis always recognized ego-defenses in the form of 'resistances' as posing an obstacle to the progress of therapy? Has it not aimed at freeing those tendencies in the patient which make for contact with and interest in other people, for expansion and growth? Is this not what really lies behind the idea of 'lifting repressions of the sexual instinct'? Freud has often pointed out that it is a serious misunderstanding to think of this as the assimilation of the ego to the id. In fact, the reverse is what he intended: where id is there ego shall be. It is equally a misunderstanding to think that this amounts to a strengthening of the ego-instincts. As Freud put it to Wortis (Wortis, 1954, p. 80): 'Analysis enriches the individual, but he loses some of his ego.'

If we look at Freud's ego-instincts in this light they seem to present a certain affinity to what Simone Weil called 'gravity' — the tendency of the ego to keep alive and enhance its power. This tendency enters into and colours every aspect of a man's life and actions, including his sexuality. If he is to find growth there, his sexuality must be purged of this tendency, it must be a form of giving, an expression of love. In Simone Weil 'gravity' is opposed to 'grace', a religious concept which is meant to signify something which comes to man from outside, from God, something which eventually kills the ego and leaves a man's will orientated in the opposite direction. She calls this orientation 'love', but she makes it clear that it is on the opposite side of the scales from 'carnal' love. Obviously Simone Weil's spirituality is alien to Freud's thought, and I do not mean to make too close a connection between them. I am merely suggesting that a comparison, however limited, between the concepts of 'ego-instincts' and 'moral gravity' helps us to see more in the Freudian concept than at first meets the eye.

Seeing more in it helps us to recognize the continuity between Freud's two instinct theories. For destructiveness is intimately connected with the ego's will to expand its domain and its reaction when thwarted or threatened. It is the desire to crush everything that gets in its way and, as such, it is an expression of the ego's will to expand, its unwillingness to contract. Thus revenge, one of the examples mentioned by Simone Weil, is a person's attempt to return the evil done to him to the person who did it. She sees it as an expression of self-assertion, an expression of the ego's unwillingness to live in a diminished domain. It is her view that it belongs to the nature of the ego to strive to expand and to resist contraction. In so far as human beings partake of this nature, what belongs to the ego is part of human nature. Simone Weil describes it as 'the mediocre part of ourselves which is almost the whole of us — which *is us*, and is what we mean when we say "I"' (Weil, 1968, p. 155).

Freud had said that 'men are not gentle creatures. . .but a powerful measure of desire for aggression has to be reckoned as part of their instinctual endowment'. The view here is that men are ineradicably aggressive *by nature*. This has been questioned by many writers: it is the way they have been brought up, the conditions under which they live that make men aggressive; to wit the gentle Trobriand islanders described by Malinowski. The sociologist Morris Ginsberg writes (1950, p. 106):

> I incline to the view that aggression is not a primary tendency to hurt or destroy, but rather an intensified form of self-assertion and self-expression, brought into play under conditions of obstruction, or of loss of independence. . .If this be so, aggression and ill-will generally may be a secondary result of thwarting and interference.

Some psycho-analysts have sided with Freud on this question, notably Melanie Klein and her followers; others have claimed that destructive tendencies are always the result of provocation. Thus Fairbairn's view that aggression is 'a reaction to the frustration of libidinal needs' (Guntrip, 1977, p. 278).

What does this conflict amount to? It is not easy to know what to make of it. Clearly Melanie Klein does not deny that aggression is intensified by 'the frustration of libidinal needs'. She speaks of the way anxiety accentuates it and 'the mutual reinforcement that is going on all the time between his (the infant's) hatred and his fear' (Klein, 1948, p. 73). Thus, in so far as what intensifies it can be removed, aggression will be reduced. She often speaks of the mitigation of hate by love. She does not think, however, that it can altogether be done away with (p. 73). Fairbairn, on the other hand, as Guntrip puts it (Guntrip, 1977, p. 344 [my italics]), 'holds that it is most important to help the patient to recognise that hate is *not the ultimate thing*, and that always love underlies hate if one penetrates deep enough'. The conflict seems to centre on whether or not aggression is innate, or whether frustration and deprivation 'originate' or 'intensify' aggression. Guntrip admits that what view one holds here makes little difference clinically (1977, p. 344).

The question of whether or not hate is 'ultimate' reminds me of the question of whether or not men are ultimately good, whether or not evil is a secondary phenomenon. I have discussed elsewhere Plato's and Simone Weil's response to the latter question (see Dilman, 1979, chapters 4, 9). It seems to me that the view which explains evil is the less deep of the two views here. Similarly it seems to me that Fairbairn's view that 'love underlies hate if one penetrates deep enough' is the less deep of the two conflicting views, especially when one admits that the question cannot be resolved by any clinical evidence. But this is not a claim about the nature of man or human nature; it is a claim about the nature of hatred and destructiveness, namely that they are not necessarily derivative phenomena. It is true that men are not born destructive, any more than they are born with love in their hearts, but their destructiveness can be as original as their love; the conflict between the two is one of the fundamental conflicts of human life at the most personal level. This is how I understand Freud's conception of the duality in man's nature. When he said that 'men are not gentle creatures. . .' he was insisting on hatred, cruelty and destructiveness as part and parcel of human life, and as expressions of a force to be reckoned with, especially at the personal, spiritual level of life. He may not have been clear in his intentions about what he wanted to say, but if taken in the way I suggest what he says does not commit him to an essentialistic view of human nature.

3 'Man as an Enemy of Culture'

Freud's view of human nature as going beyond the form in which individual men appear in particular cultures is clearly recognizable in his conception of culture and its relation to the individual. He thinks of the two as *essentially* opposed and, therefore, irreconcilable: Culture is alien to man's nature; civilization is something imposed on man. On the other side of the coin: human nature resists conforming to culture, submitting to its demands; when the individual yields, civilized behaviour necessarily remains a veneer.[3] Thus Freud says that 'every culture must be built upon coercion and instinctual renunciation' (1949e, p. 11), that 'every individual is virtually an enemy of culture' (1949e, p. 9), that 'the liberty of the individual...was greatest before any culture' (1949, p. 60), and that it is 'hard for men to feel happy in it [*i.e.* civilization]' (1949f, p. 91). 'In actual fact primitive man was better off in this respect, for he knew nothing of any restrictions on his instincts...Civilized man has exchanged some part of his chances of happiness for a measure of security' (1949f, pp. 91–2). But under the veneer of civilization men are 'savage beasts to whom the thought of sparing their own kind is alien' (1949f, p. 86).

Moral 'conventions' can at best restrain men, but they are at variance with man's nature: 'Nothing is so completely at variance with original human nature as...the ideal command to love one's neighbour as oneself' (p. 87). 'Men are not naturally fond of work' (1949e, p. 13). Hence they need a special threat or inducement to make them work. The only thing to which they take naturally is what promises some pleasure: 'The force behind all human activities is a striving towards the two convergent aims of profit and pleasure'

---

[3] Compare with Callicles in Plato's *Gorgias* (483) and Nietzsche in *Twilight of the Idols*.

(1949f, pp. 57—8). Men's 'interests in their common work would not hold them together; the passions of instinct are stronger than reasoned interests' (1949f, p. 86).

There is a great deal in this view of the interaction between human nature and culture which needs criticism and has been criticized. When Freud speaks of the state of the individual 'before any culture' he shows no recognition of the extent to which man owes his humanity to the life and culture in which he develops. Apart from this he would hardly be a person and have any autonomy to exercise. It is, therefore, nonsense to speak of him as having unrestricted freedom, as Freud does. Nor is 'primitive man', in the sense in which this phrase is normally used, less social than 'civilized man'. It is not true either that 'he knew nothing of any restrictions on his instincts'. Freud knows that this is not so, as is clear in what he wrote on the taboos that form part of the life of 'primitive man' (see Freud, 1965). If, on the other hand, Freud is referring to the so-called 'primal', 'pre-cultural' man, then this is a fiction the confusions of which Malinowski has exposed very clearly (see Malinowski, 1955, Part III). He is no man, but a pre-human anthropoid.

It has been pointed out often enough that man is a social being. Many of his aims, needs and interests, his intentions, feelings, desires and thoughts are not even conceivable apart from the life of the society to which he belongs. What significance the situations that confront him have for him, those in which he makes plans, takes decisions and acts, is determined by the life of this society. It is *he* who weighs these situations, assesses their significance; but the concepts and standards in terms of which he does so are public and are rooted in the life of the society. Similarly the intentions he forms, the decisions he takes, the feelings with which he responds to things are *his*, but the forms of life he shares with others, the activities, institutions, forms of thought that are part of these, underlie the possibility of what he wants, feels and does.

The life and culture he shares with others determine *not* what he wants, feels and does, but what he *can* want, feel and do. This life creates possibilities which become possibilities for him and also, necessarily, limits his horizons. There is no suggestion here, however, of anything being *imposed* on the individual or of his being *held back*. For when he is held back in particular cases the aspirations that are curtailed, the interests he cannot pursue, the desires he has to give up are themselves the product of the culture of the society to which he belongs. To think of culture as necessarily a form of restriction on the individual, as Freud does, is to suppose that he is an individual with aims and interests of his own independently of the culture to which he belongs — whereas I have suggested that the very possibility of his having aims and interests of his own depends on his membership of a society with its peculiar institutions, forms of life and norms of evaluation. The main question towards which I am moving here is this: is there anything that is left over to constitute a human nature which men share irrespective of the society to which they belong? If there is, how are we to understand its relation to the culture in which individual human beings find their particular identity? Is this relation wholly one of conflict and opposition?

Freud suggests that the civilization which men acquire never becomes theirs properly and that certain forms of behaviour not affected by it are natural to man or show his true nature: 'when those forces in the mind which inhibit it [i.e. the aggression which is part of men's instinctual endowment] cease to operate' men are revealed 'as savage beasts to whom the thought of sparing their own kind is alien' (1949f, p. 86). What men acquire in the process of civilization is a 'mental institution' which 'inhibits' the expression of what men are really like. When men are free from such 'inhibitions' they act 'naturally' or 'in accordance with their nature'. Thus Freud claims that the actions of the Huns under Attila, of the Mongols under Genghis Khan and Tamurlane, and of the Crusaders illustrate 'the truth of this view of man' (1949f, p. 86).[4]

For Freud the antithesis of 'in accordance with human nature' is 'imposed on the individual's will'. But, as I pointed out elsewhere (Dilman, 1979, p. 87), the question of what is external to a particular person's will is very different from the question of what is or is not in accordance with human

---

[4] Compare with Callicles' claim that the actions of Xerxes and his father when they invaded Greece and Scythia 'are in accordance with nature' (Plato, *Gorgias*, 483).

nature — whatever the latter may mean. It is a mistake to think that what conflicts with what is natural to man as such is necessarily something that conflicts with an individual person's will. A person can overcome a tendency which he shares with most other people and, in taking an action which runs counter to it, do what he wills. That is, he can be fully behind an action which conflicts with such a tendency. It would be wrong to think that such an action must be contrived or artificial.

'It is natural for men to behave as Xerxes did' does not mean that everybody in fact behaves like this, but that they *would* do so *if* left to themselves. I put it like this in analogy with Newton's notion of natural motion: a body moves naturally in the absence of impressed forces and such forces are absent only in ideal conditions — which in practice means 'never'. Similarly the idea is that men are left to themselves 'in a state of nature', i.e. in the absence of culture. But we have already seen that this idea comes from confusion. Freud, like Callicles and Nietzsche, thought of the process of acquiring a morality and becoming civilized as in some ways like the taming of a lion. But it is not true that men acquire moral values as wild animals acquire inhibitions in their training. Even when a man stops doing something he is tempted to do because it runs counter to his moral beliefs, he does not stop because his beliefs inhibit him. Moral beliefs, when they go deep, change a person's whole orientation — the way he looks at and sees things, what things mean to him, and so what he wants. They do not check him from doing what he wants. In the case of lions we can make a contrast between how they behave in their natural habitat and how they behave in captivity. We can say that how they behave in captivity is not natural to them, that they are cowed by fear of the lash and consequently unhappy. But there is no corresponding contrast in the case of human beings: morality is part of men's natural habitat, it belongs to their social environment apart from which, as I pointed out, they would not be human beings. I am not suggesting that men's social environment cannot become oppressive, but that it is not so necessarily — as Freud suggests.

I said that man is a social being and, therefore, more than a beast or animal, and I meant this as a conceptual claim. 'More than a beast' does not mean 'there is something additional in him'. It means that his life has dimensions not conceivable in an animal; that when we speak of a life with such dimensions we are no longer speaking of 'life' in the same sense as in an animal. Even if, with Freud, we could still say that there is a beast in man, it does not follow that the rest of him is somehow less real or fundamental, less part of him. So even if there is some truth in Freud's claim that as a man becomes a moral and social being something in him belonging to an earlier period is curbed or made subject to control, it does not follow (a) that this is all there was to him at the start, or (b) that what he acquires is not as much part of him, that what he becomes is not as real as what is brought under check. It does not follow that he must remain uninterested in the claims of morality. If something that takes place here is best described in terms of curbing and inhibition, much of what takes place soon goes beyond this and is best described as growth and transformation. Fairly early in this process of growth and learning the child acquires the capacity of self-control, which he acquires in harness with the capacity to speak and think. This is very different from the inhibition of a trained animal, for instance, of a dog trained to restrain its natural inclination to bite when teased. The child also acquires various motives for controlling his impulses and renouncing certain aims and desires. Thus, even if, in a particular case, when he acts from a moral motive this involves his refraining from giving in to a selfish desire, he need not be doing something contrived or less natural than seeking to satisfy the selfish desire. It is sheer sophistry to think that only what is selfish or self-seeking is natural or original.

Nietzsche thinks that a quality is not natural if 'it was not there from the beginning' (Nietzsche, p. 108). We find this same thought in Freud. But, as I have just pointed out, what was not there from the beginning may be just as real a part of the person as what was, and there need be nothing unnatural in the actions that proceed from it. This is so even when there is a conflict or opposition between what was there from the beginning and what was not.

'What was not there from the beginning and is, therefore,

new can only be something to which men do not take naturally, something that remains external to what they are really
like, something imposed on their will — the need to work, the
precepts of morality, the necessity to live with each other
and share what they have.' The complementary idea which
we also find in Freud's thinking is this: 'What does seem to
be new and not there from the beginning is only a new form
of the old, and it can only be grasped with reference to the
old.' This, too, is part of the idea that nothing new can enter
into a man's life and become genuinely his. In 'Freudianism
and Society' Anderson points out that this idea 'involves a
denial of interaction'. He describes it as 'the doctrine of. . .an
inner nature from which all characters are derived', 'the view
that the individual has his springs of action within himself'
(Anderson, 1940, p. 353). The 'inner nature' to which he
refers is Freud's 'original human nature' with which all forms
of civilized behaviour are 'completely at variance'. Anderson
points out that since interaction is a fact that cannot be denied
Freud has somehow to accommodate it, to compromise with
it (p. 353): 'The compromise made by the Freudians is to
take the earliest experiences as imposing on the original disposition modifications which are decisive for the rest of life.'
He finds this view absurd and argues that infants do not make
society but that, on the contrary, the interests, ambitions and
aspirations we find in the world of adult men come from
society and are the products of its life. A person comes to
them by sharing this life, and he has to learn a great deal to
be able to do so.

Anderson sees Freud's view that human nature and culture
stand opposed to each other as part of his 'individualism'. He
says that Freud has no sense of the individual 'as a "vehicle"
of social forces, as a member of movements which are just as
real, just as definite as he is' (p. 341). I have already agreed
with this criticism. It is perfectly true that often men fight
and hate each other because they are caught up in movements
that are themselves in conflict. They fight each other not
because *they* are antagonistic to each other, but because the
movements to which they belong are in conflict. It is *also*
true that one cannot always account for men's being caught
in movements, nor always do so in the same way. Sometimes

this is a matter of historical accident. In these movements they come into contact with ideas and develop interests that are new to them. Their way of looking at things changes, they come to have feelings about matters which could not have summoned their passions before — compassion, anger, indignation. But this process of being won over to a new movement is two-way: new possibilities are created for the individual, something new enters into his life. Equally, however, contact is made, through the movement engaging the individual, with something that is already there. In the case of the exceptional individual this may have the consequence that he brings something new to the movement, something that inspires the other members and gives the movement a new direction and perhaps new ideals.

The case of the exceptional individual and his innovations raises questions in which I am not at present interested. Anderson speaks of the individual as a 'vehicle' of social forces, and it is true that Freud lacks a sense of this. It is true, too, that this does damage not only to Freud's social philosophy, when he comments on the origins and development of social institutions and offers analyses of cultural phenomena, e.g. religious ideas and rituals, but also to his individual psychology. For in attempting to understand the individual's actions and motives, feelings and thoughts, we have to take into account something that goes beyond the individual, namely the categories of thought, the modes of significance that are rooted in the social practices in which he participates. However, it is equally true that there is a continual interaction in the life of each individual between what thus comes to his life from outside, changing him, and what it engages in him, already there.

What that which is new to his life makes of him depends as much on what he makes of it — the way he may utilize it, neutralize it, distort its significance. What he brings to the movement, his characteristic responses, come to him from other aspects of the life he takes part in, though he may have made it his and developed it in his own way. This is where his individuality lies. But these dimensions go beyond the contemporary aspects of his life, all the way back to his past, before he was an adult. This is the reverse side of the coin which one would run the risk of ignoring if one put too much stress on the individual as a 'vehicle' of social forces. The two are complementary and a great individual psychologist, as Dostoyevsky was, shows due recognition of each and of their subtle interaction, for instance, in his treatment of Raskolnikov in *Crime and Punishment*.

Men not only bring their greatness of soul to movements of which they become members; they bring also their pettinesses and immaturities. More generally, they have an 'inner', 'phantasy' life which is a heritage of their early childhood. This finds a foothold in the contemporary forms of life in which they find or lose themselves and comes into play in their individual actions as members of social movements. Thus the aggression and destructiveness which Freud has in mind when he speaks of 'the death instinct' belong to this 'inner' life; it is the inner aspect of the antagonism which members of conflicting movements feel for each other when this antagonism has 'personal animus' in it.

Anderson points out that this 'inner life' is unintelligible in separation from the 'outer', 'social' life to which the individual belongs (p. 341): 'Unless we treat a person otherwise than as a unit, unless we consider the activities which pass *through him* (in which he participates without being either *the* agent or *the* patient), we cannot even give an account of the activities which go on within him.' I agree that his interests, ideas, aims, designs, aspirations and many of his actions, i.e. much of what comes from him and goes to make up his identity as a person, cannot be understood in separation from the culture in which he has grown up and lives. So if we wish to understand how he gets caught up in movements which bring him into conflict with other men, for instance, we have to understand the interests that transcend him, the moral and political ideals which are the product not of his individuality but of his culture. We have already considered this question in our discussion of the universality of the Oedipus complex. It would be foolish to maintain that a child's phantasy life fits into a pattern that is invulnerable to cultural variations. The question is whether there is a limit to this vulnerability.

4 A Legitimate Conception of Human Nature

There is much in the claim that the culture of the society to which a man belongs makes him what he is: it does not force him into a mould from which he is constantly trying to flow out. On the other hand, it would be wrong to think that there is nothing to man other than what in him is the product of his culture.

One may wish to deny this for two different sorts of reason. First because one takes it as an expression of scepticism about the reality of the self: people are nothing over and above the social roles they play; it does not make sense to speak of their true selves. This is a distortion and a confusion,[5] and it relates to the first of the two distinctions I distinguished between at the outset of this chapter. A person's 'real character' or 'true self' is not what he shares with other human beings; it is on the contrary what distinguishes him from other people. But the above claim also relates to that and can be seen as expressing scepticism about the plausibility of discerning an a-historical aspect in human life, a limit to the cultural variations that we find among human beings.

Thus Malinowski, who criticized Freud for ignoring these variations in his 'instinct theories' and his 'doctrine regarding the development of the libido', thought that there is a limit to these variations. In both the early Freudian parts of his book and in the last part called 'Instinct and Culture', he speaks of the cultural and the innate as two independently identifiable components which enter into the constitution of an individual's personality, two components which can act in harmony or conflict with each other (Malinowski, 1955):

> We have found that at almost every step [in the growth of the average boy or girl in both societies] there are great differences due to the interplay between biological impulse and social rule which sometimes harmonise, sometimes conflict. . .(p. 71)

> In both societies, to the biological adjustment of instinct there are added the social forces of custom, morals and manners, all

---

[5] It is a distortion of the social character of human beings and of the sense in which individual identity depends on the language which a man speaks and the culture to which he belongs.

working in the same direction of binding mother and child to each other, of giving them full scope for the passionate intimacy of motherhood. . .Society co-operates with nature to repeat the happy conditions in the womb, broken by the trauma of birth. (p. 32)

In his descriptions of the different stages of childhood in the two societies compared, he says, he is concerned 'to bring out clearly the respective contributions of organism and society' (p. 52). He says that 'some of the forces by which society moulds man's biological nature [in the European and Melanesian civilizations] are essentially dissimilar' (p. 71).

It is clearly implied that there is here something which is essentially the same, namely 'man's biological nature'. The picture is the Freudian one of an instinctive 'raw material' and the 'moulding forces' which turn it into the 'finished product' we recognize in individual men. Thus in this early part of his book Malinowski speaks of the formation of the characters we find in the adults of the two societies as 'the modification in human nature brought about by the various constitutions of society' (p. 76).

In the last part of the book this picture does not disappear; but it is refined. Malinowski speaks of culture not only as curbing, channelling and moulding the natural impulses, the instinctive reactions of men, but also as creating new responses in extending, directing and transforming them. He gives special prominence to the organization of affective responses around 'definite objects', i.e. the mother, father, etc., and the formation of sentiments and personal ties. It is indeed true that, although gradual, what we have here is something momentous: the transformation of a being in many ways akin to the young of an animal, with a limited number of tendencies and reflex responses, into a human being who can think before he acts, who can control his impulses, formulate objectives, direct his actions in the pursuit of these objectives; a being furthermore whose objectives are not determined simply by the pressure of organic needs but by his interests in and sentiments for things outside himself. One could say that his life acquires many new and logically interdependent dimensions: thinking, reasoning, intentional action and willing, self-criticism, the formation of personal relations, etc. It is as a result of *learning* that a man's life comes to have these many dimensions which distinguish it from the life of an animal, which can be characterized as largely *instinctive* — both the learning and what he comes to presuppose the kind of life men live with language. Malinowski describes this transformation as 'the transition from nature to culture', 'from instinct to sentiment'.

One of the big differences between him and Freud is that for him the idea of a state of nature for man is a contradiction in terms whereas, as we shall remember, for Freud it was only in such a state that man could have the greatest liberty and find the greatest happiness. But if the possibility of such a state is ruled out by conceptual considerations, it is equally clear that the idea of culture as something alien to man's nature, and therefore necessarily opposed to it, must be untenable.

This conclusion, however, does not force us to accept a kind of 'empiricism of the affects' which not only sees man's mind as a *tabula rasa* at birth, devoid of any ideas, as John Locke insisted, but also his affective nature, thinking of all his tendencies, needs and emotions as purely products of the culture in which he develops and lives. Clearly Malinowski would not go along with such a view and he is right not to do so. But it is extremely difficult to get a proper appreciation of the interaction between 'nature' and 'culture' in the development and life of the individual, extremely difficult to keep clear of the picture of a raw material being turned into a finished product. Malinowski does not entirely succeed in doing so.

Returning to Freud, I think we can discern two different trends in his thoughts on the relation between nature and civilization, although he is not clear about their differences and runs them together. The first is the one we have criticized extensively, which sees culture and civilization as imposed on man and human nature as something that resists being civilized. The second sees man as starting life with an instinctive endowment which finds expression in certain primitive, impulsive reactions. These reactions are curbed, brought under his control, utilized, directed and transformed in the course of his interactions with other people within the kind of social setting, e.g. particular family structure, which provides the framework to these reactions. What he thus comes to is just as real as the instinctive endowment with which he starts life, or at any rate it can be. Secondly, however transformed, certain propensities remain in human life, to be reckoned with, directly related to this instinctive endowment. What Freud has in mind here has been recognized under different aspects by the greatest of moral philosophers, for instance, under the name of 'the body' or 'the flesh' by Plato.

On this latter view civilization is not something imposed on man, something alien to his nature. In the course of his development a man learns a great many things; he acquires self-control and discipline in the context of the diverse things he learns. Even in the course of play he has to check his impulses and co-ordinate his actions. This process inevitably involves some curbing of impulses, though it need not result in a loss of spontaneity. Self-discipline, as Freud himself pointed out, is not the same thing as repression. It is true that on Freud's view certain natural inclinations have to be over-come in the course of a child's development. This does not mean, however, that the process of development, in whatever form a particular culture supports, goes against the grain of human nature. For there are equally other natural tendencies which make for growth and are enlisted by those activities in which the individual develops. This is one aspect of Freud's view of the duality or bi-polarity of human nature.

On Freud's view, from the beginning, man's interaction with his environment is determined by this duality. At first this environment consists largely of his mother who attends to his needs, feeds him, comforts him and cares for him. The way he thinks of her is necessarily very different from the way he will come to think of her later. Much has to enter his life before he can do that. His life sets limits to what he can experience. These experiences are largely confined to his needs and their satisfaction, together with certain primitive emotions such as fear of loud noises, anxiety about finding the breast, greed for what it offers, anger when it is withdrawn prematurely. If after feeding he is content, he may feel his whole world to be caring, suffused with the warmth and goodness of the milk he has had. If the milk gives him wind or he is still hungry, he may cry. His whole world, as he looks at what surrounds him through his tears, may change into a cold, uncaring and hostile one. He may see it from the perspective of the anger he has felt at other times when the breast was not offered him or when it was prematurely withdrawn. He experiences the pain he feels and later his hunger, even his own choking rage, as something done to him, retaliatory in character. The world thus reflects his own anger.

Obviously how the child is treated, whether he is cared for or neglected, varies from one parent to another. The form which the caring takes — how often he is fed, when he is weaned, whether he is fed by the same person — the expectations that govern the way he is treated, all this varies from one family to another, from one society to another. These variations obviously make a difference to the affective responses evoked in the young child or infant. Nevertheless, given the narrow logical limits of what constitutes the world for him, the ingredients of this world largely transcend cultural differences. I am referring here to the world of infancy as depicted by Melanie Klein in her writings. Criticizing Freud's 'individualism', Anderson writes that infants 'are born into society, into a set of interrelated social movements, which largely determine their history' (Anderson, 1940, p. 354). Infants are born into a society, perhaps, but not into its culture. There is a sense in which an infant is hardly even born into a family. The breast that gives him milk, the arms that cuddle, warm and rock him to sleep: these are the extent of his world. Yet he does have a primitive, affective life, and it is this life which is independent at first of the culture which is soon going to shape it. Contact and interaction with his society's culture within his family is something that he comes to, and how he comes to it depends partly on the way this 'inner' life unfolds. He comes to have an 'outer' life only as he learns to speak and think so that his responses come to be mediated by the awareness of an environment that has an existence independent of his needs. It is in the course of coming to this that he also develops the capacity for intentional action and becomes a person and agent. This, I argued, takes place in the framework of modes of activity which belong to and constitute aspects of the culture of the society in which he grows up.

If I speak of the infant as having an 'inner' life before he has an 'outer' life I do not wish to deny that an 'inner' life, not expressed in words and behaviour, presupposes the possibility of its being given a recognizable expression. The 'inner' life in question here is constituted by the rudimentary beginnings of the infant's phantasy life. It does not and cannot as yet have any distinct existence from the 'natural', 'primitive', 'unlearned' reactions which I mentioned above. It is these reactions that are transformed as they become subject to the will and so stop being purely automatic reactions. If the infant were devoid of the instinctive tendencies which find expression in these reactions, the particular activities in the context of which he develops into an individual could not get a grip on him. They give him entry, as it were, into the modes of behaviour within his immediate family, and it is in these that he comes into contact with aspects of the culture of the society to which his family belongs. Yet in these reactions we find the seeds of the common humanity which lies behind the diverse forms of life we find among men.

Certainly I find no reason to suppose that there are limits to the forms of life, activity and institution that can develop where men live together. But there are limits to the kinds of quality which find expression in different forms of human activity and interaction: lust, greed, envy and jealousy, vindictiveness and revenge; love, affection, generosity and gratitude, forgiveness and the wish to make amends; anger, guilt, fear, dismay and depression; courage, devotion and self-sacrifice; cowardice, meanness and cruelty — these constitute the common humanity we find among men belonging to different cultures. This common humanity is inconceivable apart from the primitive or sophisticated cultures that have developed among men, although its seeds predate any such culture in the way I have suggested.

Here we have a positive conception of human nature, also implicit in Freud's writings, which I believe is not open to the objections I have directed to the conception Freud developed particularly in his monograph *Civilization and its Discontents*. It is a conception which becomes more prominent in the writings of Melanie Klein.

7

Development and Character

1 Development of the Individual

In his *Three Essays* Freud writes about the stages through which infantile sexuality is transformed into adult sexuality. He speaks of this as the development of the sexual instinct or libido and writes as though the concept of development in question is a purely biological one. As he puts it in his *Introductory Lectures* (p. 276): 'The sexual life. . .does not first spring up in its final form. . .but goes through a series of successive phases. . .like those in the development of the caterpillar into the butterfly.'

While there is obviously a biological aspect to what Freud is discussing, we have seen that this is not at the centre of his concern. What he is concerned with is the early emotional growth or development of the individual and the changes in the way he relates himself to his parents and other members of his family. The development of the Oedipus complex and the formation of the super-ego, as Freud saw these, belong to it. I do not see that one can treat 'the development of the libido' separately from 'the development of the ego'. Under both headings one is dealing with aspects of the development of an individual person. But what does 'development' mean here? And what do we understand by 'maturity' and by the failure to reach it?

It is not too difficult to say what these terms mean in connection with a plant, an insect or a fruit. The changes which a caterpillar undergoes in becoming a butterfly are predetermined and they take place given the right conditions. Every butterfly goes through the same sequence of changes and the butterfly is the end stage in this sequence, so we expect a caterpillar to turn into a pupa and the pupa to change into a butterfly. Development here means changing from the earlier to the later forms. A later form is more developed relative to a former one in that it comes later. Possibly, too, the butterfly may be described as 'mature' in the sense that it is only when the insect has reached this stage that it can reproduce, reproduction being singled out because of its biological significance.

We speak of development in many different connections and our use of the concept is governed by different criteria in different cases. In connection with the human body the logic of the concept is not too dissimilar from what it is in its application to plants and insects. We speak of the development of an idea, a skill, a talent, a musical theme, a relationship. Take the case of a musical theme. Obviously this is very different from the case of the butterfly. There are no regular sequences here and the generality implicit in the application of the concept is very different: it lies in the musical judgement that I make, which judgement presupposes an acquaintance with and an understanding of music in me. Similarly with the development of an idea: to appreciate the development of, say, a scientific idea, I must be acquainted with and have some knowledge of the particular branch of science in question. There is no one way in which a musical theme or a scientific idea can be developed, and there is no question of predicting any particular sequence. It takes a particular talent and imagination to develop an idea or theme in a particular field.

If a person has a particular talent and we can say that his talent is developing, we mean that he is becoming good at whatever it is he has a talent for. What counts as being good at it depends on what is in question. If the person is to become good, there is much that he will have to learn. Again this is very different from the development of a plant, the body or its organs, where obviously the changes do not presuppose any learning. Where learning comes in, the application of various criteria comes in as well, entering not merely our judgements but the development itself. Similarly, if we say that someone's powers of reasoning are developing we mean that he is learning to reason and that he can reason better now than he did previously.

If we speak of a relationship between two people as developing, again the case is different. Out of context our claim is pretty vague, but in a specific context it may mean something definite: 'The relationship is developing; it is not standing still.' We mean more than that it is simply changing, taking a different form. We may mean that the people in question are coming to know each other; perhaps that they are beginning to dispense with formalities, to drop pretences. We may mean that there is more give and take between them. We are not making a judgement about what each brings to the relationship, since this will vary with the people involved. Thus they may begin to quarrel, one of them may dominate or exploit the other. On the other hand, the quarrels may become repetitive, the relationship with all its turbulence may get into a rut. Nothing new may come into it any longer. We may then say that it has become stagnant, that it has stopped developing. But to say this takes judgement. We may say that if the relationship is to move again the people concerned will have to change their attitude towards each other, and for this they need to change in themselves. There is no goal here which the people aim to achieve, no end state towards which they either must move or want to move.

If, on the other hand, we speak of a person's moral development, then this does bring in certain value judgements. For if we say that a person is developing morally, we do mean that he is becoming a better person. This, obviously, means better from the standpoint of the speaker's values. The qualms that a person begins to have about something which he has been doing well may be seen by someone as a move towards greater moral sensibility, while someone else may see it as the loss of moral fibre in him. In this sense Freud tried to be morally neutral and to avoid making this kind of judgement.

He was concerned with the changes a person undergoes in becoming *adult* and the obstacles that impede these changes. What is in question is not physiological maturity; and the term I have used is a moral one. On the other hand, it has a fairly broad base. Its sense can be analysed in terms of such ideas as autonomy, independence and responsibility. The

changes that constitute individual or emotional development
are those that are in the direction of a greater ability to think
for oneself, to act on one's own behalf, to be more willing to
answer for what one does. Such a person may be described as
'becoming an individual', as opposed to a mere replica of his
parents. This takes courage and self-criticism, and both have
to be learned. The concept in question is broader than that
of moral development. For unless a man is himself he cannot
be a genuinely moral person. But to be himself, he must
believe in something outside himself; and it is well known
that people differ in what they believe.

There is a great deal that a child has to learn to do and to
make sense of if he is to develop in the sense under discussion.
We can say that these underlie the possibility of his growing
into adulthood. For instance, he must be able to think and
speak before he can think and speak for himself. He must be
able to act, to form intentions, before he can act on his own
behalf. To do that he must have learnt to do something when
asked to do it, and also not to do it when so told. To have
interests that he can pursue for himself there is a great deal
he must come to know and learn to understand. Similarly for
his moral convictions. A person's emotional, moral and intellectual developments go hand in hand and are different aspects
of his growth as an individual – even though in particular
cases some aspects may lag behind.

Freud takes all this for granted. He writes as a psychologist
interested in particular aspects of such a development and
not as a philosopher concerned to understand what 'development' means here. He is not clear, however, about the sense
in which the individual contributes to his own development
and about the extent to which the possibility of his doing so
depends on what comes to him from outside. He takes it for
granted that the 'healthy' child will have a thrust outward,
that he will respond to and take an interest in things outside
him, things that go on independently of his wishes. His
particular contribution lies in his study of what disturbs this
thrust outward, the anxieties that restrict his interests in
outside things, the difficulties he finds in those relations that
sustain his growth. He emphasizes how much of this comes
from the child himself, although obviously the immediate

environment to which the members of his family contribute play a part in creating problems for the growing child or in helping him to overcome those which he has.

I would say that one of Freud's contributions here lies in his emphasis on the problematic character of individual development. He thought that every individual, from childhood onward, is *inevitably* bound to meet problems and difficulties in the course of his development. He misrepresented this inevitability in the way he talked about 'instincts', although his reference to the 'duality' of man was his way of emphasizing this inevitability. He thought that growth towards autonomy and independence is a struggle with problems and difficulties in relationships. We have seen what his emphasis on sexuality amounted to in this connection. One can say that the Oedipus complex for Freud symbolizes the inevitability of conflict and difficulty. He regarded growing towards autonomy as the resolution of emotional conflict, although both 'autonomy' and 'resolution' are relative terms. I think that he regarded the idea of a 'final' resolution of difficulty as a misunderstanding. He would have said that if a person stops growing, in the sense under discussion, that is because he has got stuck, because there are certain difficulties which he is unwilling to face, and that psycho-analysis is an opening up of these difficulties with a view to enabling the analysand to start moving again.

The difficulties in question are difficulties in relationship. The analysand may feel, for instance, that those he needs most and depends on, or those he feels depend on him, prevent him from doing what he wants. His problem then will be how he can pursue his own interests without incurring their wrath, or without harming them or letting them down. He may give up what he wants, turn away from his interests, and devote himself to placating the anger of those on whom he feels dependent. On the other hand, a person may give up what he wants for the sake of someone he loves and in his devotion find a new interest.

Freud would say that where a person's commitment is based on love there is already a large part of autonomy at work — such a person depends on himself in caring for the other and it is his choice to put the other person before himself. Here we have the possibility of further growth because we have the possibility of learning. Where, on the other hand, it is anxiety that keeps a person to the course he pursues, this possibility is lacking until he wakes up to the sterility of that course and begins to feel dissatisfied. Such dissatisfaction need not be a symptom of selfishness, for he may be just as dissatisfied with his inability to give as with his failure to receive.

My main point is that where we talk of the development of an individual we are not talking of a set pattern of changes which is the lot of every individual. There may be certain landmarks fixed by the biological aspect of physical development, and there are some environmental constants which may vary from one society to another. While these play a part in determining the *form* taken by the emotional growth of the individual, that growth results from the individual's interaction with what he undergoes biologically, the expectations voiced by those around him, and the demands they make on him. What we call 'development' here is the formation of the individual and his character, 'the development of the ego' in Freudian terminology, and the individual himself contributes to it. He grows as an individual in his struggle with difficulties — in the way he meets them and in the sense he can make of what he meets in life.

The notion of development also necessarily implies a direction. In the case of moral and emotional development this direction is not determined by biological ideas but by such ideas as independence, the ability to choose freely and take responsibility for one's actions. This does not make the concept of development in question into something arbitrary. Does it depend on an allegiance to a particular set of values? In a sense it does. It depends on looking at individual human beings as having a value in themselves and not as cogs in a machine. I can imagine a society in which Freud's concept makes no sense or is rejected; a society which regards the ability to submit unquestioningly to the authority of the state as the peak of emotional and political maturity. Such a society may see any desire for independence as the expression of childish rebelliousness, and it would be short with moral and intellectual objections levelled against its views. Intellectual enquiry and free criticism, or certain forms of it, would be proscribed as objectionable, so that the question of whether *all* desire for independence can be the expression of childish rebelliousness cannot even be seriously raised. In another sense, however, Freud's concept of development is largely neutral between the competing moral values we are likely to encounter in our society. As I said, to serve most of these values and ideals a person has to be himself. Whatever the conflict between them, these values themselves demand the autonomy of the individual.

Freud believed that what divides a person impedes his ability to give the best of himself in any situation, and he saw this as a bad thing because of the value he set on the individual. He should have seen that if inner rifts that divide a person prevent him from developing into an autonomous individual, then the development he is concerned with embraces the person's interests, beliefs and commitments. If he is divided in himself, there is the danger that a commitment will be entered into for defensive purposes, or that beliefs and interests will become a vehicle for self-assertion. That is why self-criticism is so important here, the kind of criticism that asks 'What do I see in it?', 'What does it do for me?' These are *moral* questions for which there is a place in psycho-analysis. There is no reason for psycho-analysis to be hostile to such questions, not to treat them seriously.

How they are to be answered depends on the analysand's values and there is nothing in psycho-analysis to prevent a neutral treatment of these questions. Moral neutrality here, namely not interfering with the analysand in his genuine desire to straighten his relation to the values and ideals which captivate his allegiance, is perfectly compatible with moral seriousness. The analysand's desire to straighten this relation, in so far as he is troubled by it, is bound to be intertwined with his desire to straighten out his personal relationships. In both cases the analyst's role is not to legislate about the persons and values to which the analysand is related, but to help him to become critical about himself, i.e. to become clear about what he seeks, whether he has ulterior motives, what part of himself he gives and what he protects. However criticism of this sort, for which Freud's word is 'analysis', should not be confused with the kind of 'criticism' which Freud attributed to the super-ego. The latter if carping and hostile and does not come from concern. It is destructive aggression turned inwards and directed onto the self — whereas the kind of criticism that is central to psycho-analysis has no axe to grind; at any rate it should not. It can take the form of moral criticism, where the analyst enters imaginatively into the analysand's moral values while remaining detached from them. Here criticism should be contrasted with censure.

This point is connected with my discussion of Freud's concept of emotional development. For emotional development means acquiring greater autonomy, independence and authenticity, and these concepts are moral concepts — though in a broad rather than a narrowly partisan sense.

2 Character and its Defensive Role

We have seen that Freud speaks of the development of the libido, through stages, in the direction of its 'genital organization'; and he speaks of the development of the ego in the direction of 'self-mastery', that is a state in which the ego is neither a slave to the passions of the id nor acts in subservience to the super-ego. It is significant that he speaks as if the two — 'genital organization of the libido' and 'self-mastery' — coincide. It is no accident that he should have invested 'genitality' with some of the qualities that belong to self-mastery. The genital organization of the libido follows, according to Freud, the latency period and emerges out of the struggle with the Oedipus conflict. While a certain physiological development which belongs to the biology of the human body is a *sine qua non* of the emergence of a 'genital orientation', it is clear that Freud sees this orientation as something more than a susceptibility to new physical desires, something to which the individual has to win through. It is a new orientation in human relationships away from ego-centricity and dependence, to be achieved in the face of the regressive temptations inherent in the Oedipal situation. It is an orientation of the self incompatible with a pronounced ego or a severe super-ego.

Why speak of genitality at all, especially when many of those who are capable of 'genital relationships' form relationships of dependence in which they are not capable of acting with autonomy? Freud's answer is that such people's orientation is only partly genital, that it has features which belong to earlier stages of development they have not been able to outgrow — oral receptive, oral sadistic, anal erotic, phallic and urethral. While Freud certainly regarded these as biological stages, it is not clear to me how purely biological a view he took of them. Those who developed his ideas on character formation have sometimes accused him of taking a purely biological view; but the foundation of some of their later ideas was already in Freud whose perception, in my opinion, went beyond the confines of biology.

Freud's study of the formation of character, which others after him — Abraham, Ernest Jones, Wilhelm Reich, Erich Fromm, etc. — developed, is really an extension of his theories of the formation of the super-ego and the determination of its content. The super-ego is part of the ego, though a differentiated part of it. The kind of demand it makes on the ego and the manner in which the ego responds to it is certainly an important aspect of a person's character — e.g. over-conscientiousness. Freud pioneered the study of character in a paper entitled 'Character and Anal Erotism' in 1908 (1950, vol. ii), where he attempted to give an account of certain character traits along the lines he had developed in his account of neurotic symptoms. The traits in question were orderliness, parsimony and obstinacy which he traced to toilet-training in childhood and represented as 'reaction-formations' to that training. The idea is that the child minds the interference and deals with his resentment by taking the side of his parents. He staves off their displeasure by conforming and expresses his own displeasure in the ungivingness of the traits he develops. He also turns his anger back on himself in the way he keeps himself in hand and denies himself the pleasure which he would otherwise wish to seek.

The implication is that if the child had been allowed to outgrow the interests belonging to that stage of his development he would not have resorted to the reaction-formations in question. But what does 'allow' mean here? Freud would have said that if he had been encouraged to indulge in them he may have got stuck on those interests. This would contribute to the development of one form of homosexuality. Freud did not believe that discipline has no place in the bringing up of children. The important thing is that it should come from concern, have the child's welfare at heart, and be exercised with sensitivity. The reluctance to exercise authority or indulging the child are usually expressions not of concern but of conflicts and anxieties that are bound up with early deprivations and frustrations in the parent's life.

So Freud regards character as developing in what the child does in the face of certain pleasures that absorb his interest. What he does depends on his parents' attitude to these interests and on the feelings and phantasies they evoke in him. These, in turn, depend on earlier interactions. Freud's view is that, broadly, there are three ways in which the child may react. He may cling to the pleasurable activities in question and become their captive. He may swing to the opposite extreme, defend himself against indulging in them by developing traits that are antithetical to such indulgence — what Wilhelm Reich calls 'reactive character'. Such reaction-formations are at the same time a way of preserving what the child defends himself against. The reactive trait and what it puts on one side feed on each other. This state of affairs constitutes an instance of Freud's 'dynamic' conception of character. Thirdly, the child may transform the interests in question, grow out of them in their original form while still retaining something of them on which he builds — 'sublimation'.

I referred to Freud's 'dynamic' conception of character traits and mentioned the parallel he saw between them and neurotic symptoms. I do not think that this could be true of all character traits. Freud saw them 'as an expression of their libidinous source' (Fromm, 1950, p. 57). Recent American and British psycho-analysts, notably Fromm and Fairbairn, have criticized him. But before we can consider their criticism we must ask what is to be understood by character. Psycho-analysts generally have in mind the relatively permanent forms of behaviour, ways of orientation, and types of relationships characteristic of a particular person. In combination they make up one aspect of the person's individuality. They are what we mention in answer to the question: 'What is he like?' This question should be distinguished from another question which concerns his identity and which only he can ask himself: 'Who am I?' This latter question relates to his roots and allegiances and the place he has given them in his life. Character traits are those aspects of a man's personality which he has acquired in the course of his interactions with people from very early life onwards — in contrast, for instance, with his temperament which is determined by aspects of his inherited physiological make-up. Of course, temperament too plays a part in the formation of character since it enters into a person's interactions with other people.

Freud held that character is more or less permenently fixed in the first four to six years of life and constitutes a mould which shapes what a person acquires in his later life. He will certainly develop new interests as a result of what he meets in his later life, enter into new activities, learn patterns of behaviour that belong to these, assimilate new values and be attracted by new ideals. All this will inevitably shape him in new ways. It is Freud's contention, however, that what the individual comes to acquire in this way will continue to bear the imprint of his old character. For instance, his egocentricity will carry through into the way he relates himself to the new values he acquires. In whatever interest he takes up his pride and ambition may come to dominate his activities and refuse to let him go even when he fights them.

Freud did not think that a person's development stops once his character is formed; but he thought that it sets limits to this development, that it determines the form which that development takes. Obviously, whether or how much a person's character actually restricts his development depends on the kind of character he possesses. If a person had no character, in the way that a chameleon has no colour of its own, then I do not see how he could make anything his own and grow.

It is the tenacity with which a person's character clings to him so much of the time and resists his attempts to change it that must have impressed Freud. It lies at the core of his 'dynamic' conception of character. As Fromm puts it (1950, p. 56): 'Freud recognised. . .that the character structure of a person represents a particular form in which energy is canalized in the process of living'; and so the study of character, as Balzac put it, deals with 'the forces by which man is motivated'. Of course, talk about 'energy' and 'forces' here, and even about the way a person's character 'clings' to him, is metaphorical language — which is not to say that it should be rejected. On the contrary, it needs to be weighed and understood: what does it come to and how much does it illuminate? I believe that Wilhelm Reich's perceptive study of character in his book *Character Analysis* throws light on both the value of this approach and on its limitation.

Reich's analysis of character follows Freud's lead and develops his suggestions. Like Freud he sees character traits as deriving from phases in 'the development of the libido' and thinks of what determines their form as ranging between 'the sublimation of the libido' and 'a reaction-formation against it'. Sublimation leaves the child accessible to contact and experience, and so permits growth. Reaction-formation, on the other hand, is a defensive measure and constitutes a way of clinging to a particular position. Someone whose character contains reaction-formations remains relatively closed to contact and starved of spiritual nourishment. Reich also contrasts types of character which date back to phases of pre-genital organization and 'genital character'. The modes of behaviour and orientation typical of the former are 'infantile' and 'narcissistic'. Only those typical of the latter are 'mature', representing growth in the direction of autonomy. Thus, contrast the friendliness of 'the oral-receptive character' with that of 'the genital character'. The first is naive and expectant; it thrives on being fed. When disappointed it easily gives way to despair. The latter is staunch and giving. It can certainly be hurt, but it is not self-centred.

Reich's study of character centres around three questions, each of which calls for some philosophical scrutiny: (a) 'The function of character formation': 'Why a character is formed at all and what is its economic function?' By 'economic' Reich means 'having to do with the distribution of energies'. (b) 'Conditions of character differentiation': Why is this type of character formed rather than that? (c) The differences between genital and pre-genital character structures. Reich accepts Freud's theory of character formation but he classifies character in terms of clinical features. He is concerned with character structures as they obstruct analysis and thus refers to the pre-genital forms of character as 'neurotic' character structures. They incorporate the very difficulties for which psycho-analysis offers help. Hence the importance of 'character analysis' in the course of treatment to which Reich's book makes an important contribution. Needless to say we should not confuse 'character analysis' in this sense with the analysis of the concept of character to which Reich's book also makes a contribution.

Why is a character formed at all? If we are to make sense of this question we have to enter into Reich's thinking. He reminds us that popularly we speak of people as hard or soft, proud or humble, cold or warm. But it soon becomes clear that he is thinking primarily of such cases as those in which we say of a man that he is haughty, for instance, in order to keep people at a distance, and that underneath this exterior he is sensitive to being slighted. Yet this exterior is very much part of him; it is not something from which he can separate himself. It is in fact part of what he is like: his character. This character trait is what he has developed to protect himself from hurt and from the anxiety which his vulnerability to it provokes — hence Reich's idea of 'the function of character formation'. Reich does not suggest that one can explain *all* character traits in *this* way; but his main interest centres on those that can be so explained. Their responsiveness to psycho-analysis goes with this.

The contrast in question is this. One man may be polite because he has been well brought up and is of a friendly disposition. In another man politeness may cover aggression and hide the anxiety he feels about this aggression. This second man's politeness will be exaggerated and stiff. It will assume a certain urgency where he meets rudeness and unfriendliness. It is something without which he doesn't know how to get on and feels exposed. It is also bound up with what the second man has learned; it comes to him from the way he has been brought up. But he is related to it differently from the way the first man is. We could say that in the first man politeness is part of the way in which he relates to other people; it characterizes the form which his relationships take. At the heart of it is consideration of other people. In the second man it is a way of dealing with the anxiety to which these relationships expose him. It represents an orientation centred on this anxiety rather than on the people who are its recipient. As such it is a barrier to contact with them.

This is the kind of case on which Reich's conception of character as a defensive device or protective armour is model-led. The more a person needs to protect himself, e.g. from anxiety, the less vitality he has left at his disposal, since it is taken up in maintaining the mode of behaviour and thought that forms part of his character. In the story 'St. Mawr' D.H. Lawrence speaks of what Reich calls 'character armour' as 'attitude' (Lawrence, 1934, pp. 566–7): 'She realised that, with men and women, everything is an attitude only when something else is lacking. Something is lacking and they are thrown back on their own devices.' These are the devices of the ego — the ego as mediator or negotiator (See Freud, 1933, p. 108). What is lacking is what is 'bound' in a reactive charac-ter structure, what has been 'repressed', rendered inoperative. While it is kept in this frozen state the person cannot find what he wants, he cannot act on his own behalf. While he is absorbed in defending himself, he cannot find much interest in his surroundings, enthusiasm for projects that involve other people or joy in commerce with them. In short, he cannot give himself, much of him is not there to do so: 'This armour inevitably means a reduction of the total psychic mobility' (Reich, 1950, p. 145).

Reich thus draws attention to the way in which the de-ployment of a man's vitality in his character impoverishes him. Professor Macmurray says of such a man that if he is 'significant' this is not because he is 'vital'. He is 'significant' through the particular qualities that he possesses as accomplish-ments — his wit, for instance, or his erudition. He is dispersed in these qualities; you don't notice him so much as his quali-ties — not because he is self-effacing but because he is self-absorbed. Macmurray is thinking of an extreme case (see Macmurray, 1933, pp. 153–4). In the lives of the people Reich has in mind, there are areas which do not offer them any threat. Feeling safe here they can redeploy the energies used up in maintaining their character armour and give themselves to what interests them. In these restricted areas they put more of themselves into their responses in terms of gaiety, enthusiasm, appreciation, admiration, gratitude, devotion and warmth, as well as in terms of anger, dejection and grief. Reich talks here (1950, pp. 145—6) of 'the mobility of the armour' and, where these areas have become permanent, he talks of 'gaps in the armour'. He says that 'the degree of character mobility, the ability to open up to a situation or to close up against it, constitutes the difference between the healthy and the neurotic character structure.' Where the armour is up, any situation that tends to obstruct a person's customary approach, to neutralize his responses, will provoke anxiety and redouble his efforts to keep to the way he is. This will bring home to him how little he knows how to be any other way, how difficult he finds it to bend, how ill-fitted he is to operate outside the narrow confines of his everyday life: 'Nosy was frightened all right, out of his wits, but not out of his character, which was just the same, only more so. Devoted and pig-headed. As if hammering made it tougher' (Cary, 1961, p. 160).

'Safe' and 'dangerous' here are to be understood with reference to early conflicts and anxieties which have influenced character formation. Such conflicts can, of course, be resolved, but for this the child has to be prepared to *move*: he may have to give up something he wants, forgive those whom he feels have wronged him. To cling to a desire, to nurse a grudge are instances of immobility in developmental terms. The child's unwillingness to move may come from the craving to indulge his desires, from resentment, and again from an inability to tolerate feelings of deprivation, anxiety and guilt, or a combination of these. Reactive character structures enshrine these forms of immobility and keep a person locked in inner conflict. The task of analysis, where such structures are prominent, is to help the analysand to dispense with the protection he gets from them so that the conflicts they cover up can be exposed to analysis. Only then can he begin to move again, reconsider his relation to the past, change his orientation towards the present.

'Character armouring is, on the one hand, a *result* of the

infantile sexual conflict and a mode of solving it' (Reich, 1950, p. 148). Reich means that it is an attempt to come to terms with the conflict. It does not solve it, however, it merely buries it alive (p. 156): 'The basic infantile conflict continues to exist, *transformed into chronic attitudes*, into chronic automatic modes of reaction from which the infantile conflict must be analytically uncovered.' Not only is the conflict not solved, but as each layer of the character armour is formed, it creates new conflicts and new problems. These in turn become the basis of new character formations, new layers being added to the character armour. Among these problems is the building-up of anxiety which has itself to be absorbed into and bound by the successive layers of character formation. That is why where the analyst refuses to fall in with the analysand's character-defenses the analysand's anxiety mounts up.

Reich mentions the role not only of 'reaction-formation' but also that of 'introjection' and 'identification' in the formation of character.[1] The child takes on various aspects of his parents' character, their anxieties and their defenses, and makes them part of himself. This is partly a sympathetic identification from which the imitation of their behaviour flows, and partly a defensive one designed to keep at bay and control unruly aspects of himself which bring him into conflict with his parents. What he thus makes part of himself goes to make up what Reich calls the 'content' of his character (1950, p. 160): 'The character of the ego consists of various elements of the outer world, of prohibitions, instinct inhibitions and identifications of different kinds. The contents of the character armour, then, are of an external, social origin.'

In short, Reich's answer to the question, 'Why is a character formed at all and what is its economic function?' is this: character is a permanent modification in behaviour and orientation formed at a time when the child is weak and defenseless. It is formed in the course of a struggle with conflict and difficulties. The kind of danger from which the child tried to protect himself lies in the consequences of giving in to his passions and inclinations. These consequences include

---

[1] Freud made use of these notions in his account of the formation of the super-ego.

punishment, loss of love, real and imaginary injuries to loved ones. As Reich puts it (pp. 160—61):

> The necessity of repressing instinctual demands gives rise to character formation. . .The character, once formed, makes a great deal of repression unnecessary; this is possible because instinctual energies which are free-floating in the case of simple repression, are absorbed in the character formations themselves. The establishment of a character trait, therefore, indicates the solution of a repression problem: it either makes the process of repression unnecessary or it changes a repression, once established, into a relatively rigid, ego-accepted formation.

In this way defense and repression become part of the orientation of the ego and not something which the ego has to suffer like 'neurotic symptoms'. So the 'function' of character is (a) to avoid the dangers I have mentioned and the anxiety provoked by them; (b) to absorb the 'secondary' anxiety produced by facing life under its handicap; (c) to use the energy or vitality that lies in the passions thus kept at bay to seal them off. Reich's view is that such a deployment of this vitality decreases the frustration which the person experiences in resisting those passions and repressing them. This is directly connected with Freud's view of the ego's use of the id's energy and is what Reich has in mind when he speaks of the 'economic function' of reactive character.

3 *Character Differentiation and Erotogenic Interest*

On what does the fact that a person has the character he has as opposed to another depend? Why is he quarrelsome, for instance, rather than its opposite, the kind of person who wants to keep peace at any price? Why is he aggressively self-assertive rather than timid and retiring? Why is he moody, prone to depression, rather than steadily over-optimistic? My choice of examples is deliberate and is meant to reflect Reich's interest in reactive forms of character. As he puts it (p. 145): 'Exaggerated politeness in one person is no less motivated by anxiety than is harsh or brutal behaviour in

another person.' Thus he seeks to understand why, for instance, two people react in opposite ways to the same stresses
and anxieties and develop forms of character that are diamet-
rically opposed to each other.

Other questions under the same heading have to do with
'developmental weaknesses of character': Why is his friendliness not as steady as another's? Why is his generosity not as
thoughtful of others as it could have been? Here we are not
dealing with forms of protection. Reich connects weaknesses
that characterize one form of friendliness or generosity, in
distinction from others, with what has impeded emotional
development at some early stage. A lot of things would have
to have come together for a person to be able to make a
reliable and resourceful friend, and some of these may have
remained undeveloped.

What about the strengths that distinguish one form of
character from another? Reich does not consider this question.
But the light which psycho-analysis can throw on this question
can only be a limited one. It can certainly throw light on the
good influences in a person's childhood, environmental and
temperamental, which help to overcome his early greeds and
jealousies, to tolerate anxiety rather than evade it. The
assumption is that some conflict and difficulty is inevitable,
and that some greed, envy, hatred, guilt, fear and anxiety
enters every child's life.[2] Within reason these are a spur to
development and are part of what develops grit in character.
However, this falls very much short of explaining the strengths
of a person, or 'the development of character' in the sense in
which Freud once used this term when he said (Wortis, 1954,
p. 129): 'The reason for so much bad science is not that talent
is rare, not at all; what is rare is character. People are not
honest, they don't admit their ignorance, and that is why
they write such nonsense.' He had in mind what it takes for a
man to rise above mediocrity. I doubt that one can explain
what enables a man to do so, any more than one can explain
what enables a writer to develop style.

Neither Freud nor Reich deny the reality of 'moral educa-

---

[2] This is what in the previous chapter I characterized as Freud's positive legitimate
conception of human nature.

tion', direct or indirect, from childhood onwards — for instance, teaching the child to consider other people, to share his toys with his brothers and sisters. Teaching here does not mean showing him the way to do something which he wants to do, but getting him to want to do it. It is an education of the will and of the emotions. How is that possible? This is a philosophical question which neither Freud nor Reich discusses. They know that virtues of character cannot be imposed on the child from outside and that even providing the child with a source of inspiration can be premature and has its dangers. Freud is suspicious of educational ambition in the parents and believes in the importance of providing a child with stability in his everyday life, support and understanding in his difficulties. As for the teaching and training, and the framework of discipline within which these take place, psycho-analysts remind us that these belong to the relationship between the child and his parents. They stress the importance of what goes on below the surface for understanding how much the child can take of what is offered and what he can make of it. Hence the relevance of the child's unconscious conflicts, his ways of coping with them, and also the spirit in which his parents teach, encourage, and discipline him. If, for instance, a child is to be taught obedience and see some virtue in it, he will have to be encouraged to be independent. Otherwise he will either resent it and grow rebellious, or he will develop a reaction-formation in the form of a submissive docility. In either case his will remains unbending.

I said that where moral education and character building is concerned the educator has to get the child to *want* to do something. Obviously he has to present it in a certain light, a light in which it is attractive to the child, appeals to something in him. But if the child is to take what is offered, the educator has to leave it to the child and be genuinely prepared for him not to take it. The child must feel that the educator has nothing personally at stake except his concern for the child, which means that he must himself be free from inner conflicts that date back to his own childhood.

It is an assumption we find in both Freud and Reich, for which I believe there is justification, that all learning, however much it may be motivated by genuine interest, involves some curbing and frustration, and that while this need not create inner conflict, it can easily do so. Reich believes that in the case of the immature child it is bound to create some conflict (1950, p. 149): 'Character formation depends not merely on the fact that instinct and frustration create a conflict; it depends also on the nature of this conflict, on the period at which the character-forming conflicts occur, and on what impulses are involved.' He sets out the following schema (p. 150):

The result of character formation depends on the following factors:

1 The time at which an impulse is frustrated;
2 The extent and the intensity of the frustrations;
3 Against which impulses the central frustration is directed;
4 The ratio between permission and frustration;
5 The sex of the main frustrating person; and
6 The contradictions in the frustrations themselves.

By 'impulse' Reich means an emotion, inclination or interest. His view is that at an early age its prohibition results in repression and the opportunity for the child to outgrow or 'sublimate' it is lost. This lays the ground for a reaction-formation. So the child has to be helped to outgrow it and if he is spoilt, indulged, and the prohibition comes at a later time, the conflict will reach stalemate (p. 151): 'The basis is laid for the development of an impulsive character.' Psychopathic character constitutes an example. Reich writes (p. 151): 'In the impulsive character it is not the reaction-formations which are used as a defense against the impulses; rather, the impulses themselves, especially sadistic impulses, are utilised as a defense against imaginary dangers, including the danger threatening from the impulses.'

Such a person is very far from any kind of autonomy and self-mastery. He is at the mercy of the impulses triggered off by situations which assume an emotional significance for him through the unconscious phantasies they stir up. These phantasies are an expression of the state of dependence at which he has remained stuck. The 'instinct-inhibited character' presents the opposite picture with his rigidity, remoteness and lack of emotions. Such people, Reich points out, are submissive and uncritical and equally far from autonomy. This, relatively speaking, is true also of forms of 'reactive character'.

I will not follow Reich into the details of his interesting discussion and illustration of the influence of the rest of the six factors he has listed on character formation. In connection with 'the sex of the main frustrating person' he discusses the role of identification in character formation and the way the character traits of parents are passed on to the children, how a child can become like one of the parents or unlike him or her, and the way this affects his sexual orientation. He mentions, for instance, the case of the boy whose mother is very strict while his father is a weak disciplinarian. Such a boy will identify himself with his mother. How this affects his character depends on the developmental phase at which the identification occurs. An identification with the mother 'on a phallic basis' will make the boy narcissistic and sadistic. When he grows up he wants to be admired by women and is cruel to them. Reich points out that this character protects him from his own tender feelings for women (p. 153). An earlier identification with the mother 'on an anal basis', however, leads to the development of a passive attitude towards women. An exaggerated severeness of the father can also lead to such an identification with the mother. Here the boy gives up his masculinity and retreats to a passive-feminine attitude towards first the father and, later, towards all persons in authority. But, as Reich puts it, though 'he *is* feminine' nevertheless 'he *wants to be* masculine'. 'This tension between a female ego and a masculine ego-ideal results in a severe feeling of inferiority.' He cannot realize his 'father-identification in the superego. . .because of the lack of phallic position' (p. 153). In contrast 'the phallic-narcissistic character wards off his inferiority feeling successfully so that it is visible only to the trained observer' (p. 154). Reich considers other examples as well: the hysterical character of women who repeatedly flirt with men but shrink back when the situation threatens to become serious, the character of women who develop a sticky attitude towards older women to whom they attach themselves in a masochistic manner.

He brings out well the subtle two-way relation between the

form of a person's sexual orientation and his character. Although he uses Freud's theory of the development of the libido through the successive promimence of different erotogenic zones in his account of 'character differentiation', he puts emphasis on the interaction between the child's erotogenic preoccupations and his relationships with his parents, the mutual influence of one on the other. As I said before, the one-sided emphasis of Freud on the role of the prominence of erotogenic zones in the child's emotional development has come under severe criticism from several quarters in psycho-analysis. Such criticism, as I see it, is part of the development of Freud's ideas rather than their rejection. This progress is already visible in Reich who, at the time he published *Character Analysis* in 1933, was still very close to Freud's views — although later he was to depart from them in radical ways. Before I turn to the way Reich contrasts the 'genital' and 'pre-genital' characters, let me briefly consider the criticism of Freud's emphasis on erotogenic zones to which I have just referred.

Erich Fromm who, advisedly, drops the terms 'genital' and 'pre-genital' in his classification and discussion of character, nevertheless retains the developmental distinction in both Freud and Reich between mature and immature forms of character. He writes (1950, p. 57): Freud 'interpreted the *dynamic nature* of character traits as an expression of their *libidinous source*. The progress of psycho-analytic theory led. . .to a new concept which was based, not on the idea of a primarily isolated individual, but on the relationship of man to others.' We have met this criticism earlier in our considerations of Malinowski and we have seen how far it is justified. A similar criticism comes also from the opposite quarter in psycho-analysis — opposite to those psycho-analysts, like Karen Horney and Erich Fromm, who have adopted a 'sociological orientation'. I am thinking of Fairbairn. His view on this point is put succinctly by Harry Guntrip as follows (Guntrip, 1977):

> The infant is not immature because he is oral; he can as yet be no more than oral because he is immature, and at first capable only of taking without giving. . .The adult is not mature because genital,

but is capable of proper genital relationships because mature (p. 291). The anus is only an artificial, not a natural, libidinal organ, just as faeces are only a symbolic, not a real, libidinal object. Usually anal functioning is endowed with emotional significance because the mother forces it into the centre of her relationship with the child. Since the transitional stage consists of the struggle to outgrow infantile dependence on the mother primarily, it oscillates between rejection and retention of objects, both processes being easily symbolised anally. . .Fairbairn rejects the idea of a biological anal phase, and regards anal phenomena as simply dramatisations of conflicts concerning internalised objects in the transitional stage (p. 292). What we do at each developmental stage with bodily organs such as the mouth, anus and genital is determined by the quality of our personality and personal relations at each stage, rather than *vice versa* (p. 293).

Compare and contrast with Malinowski writing as an anthropologist. They both emphasize the importance of the child's relationships, the way he is treated by his parents and the way the child reacts to this treatment. But while Malinowski stresses the membership of the parents to a particular society, the way this determines their treatment of the child, and the way he is formed in becoming a member of that society, Fairbairn is interested in the way in which give and take between parents and children is profoundly influenced by the parents' inner conflicts and the child's unconscious phantasies. There is no incompatibility between these two approaches and I see them as complementary.

8

Character and Maturity

1 Forms of Infantile Character

Freud's and Reich's view is that character is formed in the course of the child's emotional growth. Such growth involves learning a great many things and includes learning to control and give up passionate desires and sensual inclinations. The child learns to do so partly in response to demands made on him and standards to which he is expected to conform. He does so also in conformity to his own desires and expectations. For instance, he may learn to control his rage because he does not want to hurt those he loves. Some children find it relatively easy to learn to control their anger, to give up their greed, to make amends, to forgive, to outgrow their hatred, to face anxiety without resorting to defensive measures. Others find it hard: they cling to their inclinations in defiance, or resort to defensive measures which burden them when they face new situations. This holds them back and distorts their development. Thus think of the way someone with a chip on his shoulder faces a new situation. It is not too difficult to see that what he can find in that situation, what he can contribute to it, and what he can learn in the process, will be distorted by the resentment he brings to it and the presuppositions with which he comes to it. In the case of the child the defiance with which he refuses to move, and the defensive measures to which he resorts, lead to the development of a protective form of character. The responses that are in character in such a case are dictated more by inner needs and necessities that have become permanent than by what he finds in the situations to which the responses are directed. Such a person's responses are relatively set, stereotyped, scripted in advance, the opposite of spontaneous.

This is not what the expression 'in character' means, but it is the form which being in character takes where character has become a straightjacket, an 'armour' as Reich calls it. Here a person's character, although it is the aspect under which he appears and is known, represents not the way he is, but the way he feels he *has* to be. However, a person's character can, of course, come more or less near to representing the way he is. Here we may talk of authenticity and autonomy — the two go together. Reich and Freud talk of the 'genital' orientation, Erich Fromm talks of 'the productive character', and Fairbairn talks of 'mature dependence' in contrast with 'infantile dependence'. These are all developmental concepts. Reich describes the various pre-genital and reactive forms of character as 'neurotic' and 'infantile'. The idea is that the *apparent* orientations which constitute such characters are false and defensive, and the *real* orientations they hide are those that belong to different stages of childhood. They conflict with the adult aspirations of the person himself and the adult expectations of the people to whom he is related as friend, colleague, acquaintance, neighbour, husband or wife, parent, teacher, adviser, etc. The more 'reactive' such a character is the more prominent are its *defensive* aspects. The more 'impulsive' it is the more prominent will be its *infantile* orientation. Reich, in common with other analysts, would say that many of the defenses characteristically used by a person date back to childhood and were developed in the face of responses directed to him as a child. He also thinks that impulsive aspects of character often themselves have a defensive role. In other words, the categories of 'defensive' and 'impulsive' are not exclusive.

Although an impulsive person may be described as 'spontaneous', in contrast with 'controlled' or 'calculating', impulsiveness is not the same thing as spontaneity. A person can be spontaneous without being impulsive. But if a grown-up person has remained childish, his spontaneity will be impulsive. Obviously where impulsiveness shades into compulsion we shall no longer be justified in speaking of spontaneity. One has to distinguish between the kind of control that is grounded in fear and is defensive, even when it is at the service of a positive ambition, and the kind of control which is an expression of self-mastery. In Freud's terminology, in the first case the ego is in the service of the super-ego, in the second case it is its own master. In the first case it is being controlled, in the second it is in control. Where it is not in control, it is ruled by the id. Reason weighs relatively little with such a person; the fear of frustration looms so large for him that he cannot give sufficient attention to considerations of reality, take them into account in his actions. He has not learned to do so: he has not developed a sense of responsibility. This is the impulsive character. He is the opposite of the reactive character, though equally infantile in developmental terms.

Between these two poles we have positive orientations that are also infantile in their dependence or narcissism – people with a voracious greed, an ambition that takes the form of the desire to excel others, excessive envy, vanity or cruelty. Such character forms are not necessarily defensive, and there need be no sharp discrepancy between the way such a person is and the way he appears to be. Yet we cannot say of him that he has found himself, that he is himself. We can only say: 'This is the way he is: envious or greedy. But in his envy or greed he is not himself.' Here 'not being oneself' means 'not having reached autonomy'. For the sake of convenience we can describe these character forms as narcissistic.

Thus I distinguish between *reactive, narcissistic* and *impulsive* forms of character. The line between them is by no means sharp, and in the borderline region between narcissistic and impulsive forms of character we have traits of character we single out and name, such as recklessness, irresponsibility, cowardice, which have their source in a disturbed sense of identity. They are negative character traits, in the sense that darkness is the absence of light. To attribute such traits to a person is to imply that he lacks something – prudence and thoughtfulness, responsibility and concern, courage – something that has not developed in him.

Reich's primary interest in *Character Analysis* is in the defensive role of character in psycho-analytic treatment and in the analysis of the resistance it offers to the progress of such treatment. Thus he concentrates on reactice character and the loosening of the character armour. The patient clings to his 'armour' out of anxiety; to give it up means facing anxiety and also often guilt and depression. He clings to his narcissistic trends, on the other hand, because he is unwilling to give up what he gets out of the pursuit of those activities which constitute the active expression of these trends. Often unwillingness itself comes from a fear of facing the void which giving them up would leave in his life. But to cling to them is to resist a different orientation, one excluded by narcissism, which would make it possible for something new to enter his life, something which would enable him to grow. I am thinking primarily of something that is both forward and backward looking, a concern for people that encompasses his past relationships as well as his present ones, a concern which leaves him vulnerable to sorrow, guilt, grief and depression. The questions raised by the analytic modification of these aspects of character do not figure prominently in Reich's book. These are questions to which psycho-analysis has returned in its more recent developments.

If I go along with most psycho-analysts in describing these forms of character as 'infantile', it is important not to confuse them with their adult forms. Thus, for instance, confidence in one's beliefs should not be confused with dogmatism which is a reactive character trait that hides doubt. Over-politeness, as we have seen, is not the same thing as the politeness of a well-brought-up person. It is a reaction-formation which serves to keep hostility under control. Greed which can characterize a person's eating habits, his sexuality, or his ambitions, is not the same thing as a 'healthy appetite'. It springs from early emotional deprivation and the anxieties aroused by it. Over-ambitiousness often stems from such greed and the envy that grows out of its frustration. It is also often an attempt to compensate for one's doubts regarding one's inner resources. But not all ambitions are self-seeking, some have at their centre a genuine interest in something outside the self. While these are relatively rare, at least in their pure and unadulterated form, such ambitions are not expressions of an ambitious character. We use other terms to describe the character of people who have them, for instance 'dedicated', meaning capable of dedication.

Recklessness or bravado, which may be confused with courage, are not at all the same thing. The former comes from an unawareness of the reality of danger, an inability to attend to it or take it seriously. It is a form of irresponsibility. Bravado is a compensatory trend, like boasting. Courage, on the other hand, as Plato has pointed out more than once, implies a full awareness of danger and does not exclude fear. When we describe a courageous man as 'fearless' we mean that he has overcome his fear. In the light of what he attends to and cares for it is reduced to relative insignificance — much in the way that what Kant called 'the dear self' is of little significance for the person we describe as 'self-forgetful'. In contrast, fear dominates the consciousness of the coward to the point of paralysis. Cowardice is not, of course, an 'infantile' form or trait of character as such, but a lack of moral achievement (not in the sense of accomplishment) bound up with a failure in emotional development. The man who cannot bring himself to face danger is in some ways like a man who cannot remain loyal to his friends or beliefs in adverse circumstances. What it takes to be courageous and loyal cannot be found in a dependent or narcissistic orientation of will.

Again, there are forms of friendliness and love, passive or possessive, which are distinguished by the dependent attitude at their centre. They are based on the person's needs and are fed by what the person receives. A mature form of friendliness or love on the other hand, while it may not be indifferent to what it receives from the other person, is above all giving. Even the appreciation and gratitude with which it responds to what it receives is outgoing and giving. Similarly for meekness and obedience, which have a mature as well as an immature face. An obedient person who simply takes his guidance from those in authority may be someone who has abdicated the power to think and to take decisions for himself, one who has not developed this power. He finds it easy to let others take care of him. His trust in them is uncritical, and his obedience is a form of passivity. Alternatively his obedience may be servile and ingratiating, meant to provide him with an identification with someone who possesses inner strength; or it may be a form of submissiveness which is a reaction-formation against hostility and rebelliousness. There is, on the other hand, the kind of obedience which comes from strength and involves no relinquishment of autonomy. Here one should not forget that it is possible to renounce the self, in the sense demanded by some religions, without relinquishing one's autonomy.

Earlier I distinguished between ambition and ambitiousness. One can make a similar distinction between rebellion and a rebellious character. A person can rebel against some form of evil — oppression, tyranny, injustice. This implies regard for something outside the self and takes courage. We sometimes describe a person as a 'rebel', meaning that he is not like a sheep and has a highly developed sense of independence. A rebellious person, on the other hand, is one who cannot go along with any scheme that he has not initiated or submit to authority for fear of losing his independence. His rebelliousness is a way of bolstering up his independence which unconsciously he feels to be precarious because threatened by a deeper form of dependence.

Thus dependence and independence, in terms of which many psycho-analysts have tried to distinguish between maturity and immaturity, have themselves many faces. There is, for instance, an aggressive form of independence which betrays an inner fear of dependence and loss of personality; and there is a form of dependence in which a person is willing to depend on something or someone other than himself without feeling that this threatens his autonomy. This latter form of dependence takes courage and trust and, in some cases, patience. Both Kierkegaard and Simone Weil have described religious forms of it. When Fairbairn speaks of 'mature dependence' he has in mind more mundane varieties of this kind of dependence. His point is this: we have to rely and depend on people for so many things so much of the time. If this makes us uneasy, then it is because it tempts us to regress to an earlier mode of dependence and to exploit the situation. This temptation in turn threatens us with a feeling of helplessness from which our 'mature orientation' shields us. Thus the apparently mature trends in our character

may themselves have a role akin to what Reich calls a character armour. What Fairbairn calls 'mature dependence' is the
ability to depend on others, especially in a close relationship
such as marriage, without feeling threatened. Thus in a crisis
a man or wife may come to his partner for comfort, like a
child, or during a holiday or festivities let his hair down
without being afraid that he will never be able to get a grip
on himself again or recover his poise. If he cannot do without
his poise, then he must be needing it badly. As Reich puts it
(1950, p. 169): 'He can, under appropriate conditions, be
childlike but he will never appear infantile; his seriousness is
natural and not stiff in a compensatory way because he has
no tendency to show himself grown-up at all costs.'

Reich describes this in terms of 'character mobility: the
ability to open up to a situation or to close up against it'
(p. 145). 'The ego of the genital character also has an armour,
but it has the armour at its command instead of being at its
mercy. . .The pliability as well as the solidity of his armour
are shown in the fact that he can open up to the world as
intensely in one case as he can shut himself off from it in
another' (p. 169). He is not afraid to say 'Yes', not afraid to
say 'No'. When he says 'Yes' he is not submissive, when he
says 'No' he is not defiant. Reich goes on (p. 169): 'In the
sexual act with the loved partner. . .the armour is temporarily
dissolved almost completely, the whole personality is engulfed
in the pleasurable experience, without any fear of getting lost
in it.'

My point is that it takes both courage and strength to be
vulnerable, not to have to protect oneself. People are generally
afraid that others will take advantage of this, or that it will
leave them utterly dependent and at their mercy. The fear is
not simply that others will harm them, but that they will
themselves exploit other people's goodness and continue to
want to feed on it. It is this latter desire which is an expression
of what Fairbairn calls 'infantile dependence'. People who are
relatively free from it, in the sense of having grown out of it,
and who are able to exercise discrimination and can trust
others, can in certain situations accept a dependent role
without the fear of being submerged, engulfed, or of losing
their identity. This is not the same thing as what Reich has in

mind when he speaks of opening up to a situation. But many people fear it lest it degenerates into a form of dependence once they are on the slippery slope of regression. That is why the kind of independence that is rigid and brittle signifies that the subject has not outgrown an earlier form of dependence which frightens him. It is a way of resisting its pull; that is why it betrays some immaturity in him. It is for this reason that Fairbairn prefers to characterize genuine maturity in terms of the kind of dependence he characterizes as 'mature'. Given that one can explain the difference between the two forms of dependence this characterization involves no circularity. In his discussion of Fairbairn's ideas Guntrip writes (1977, p. 383):

> Dependence is, in fact, an ineradicable element in human nature, and the whole development of love and the affections arises out of our needs for one another. . .Without the acceptance of that measure of dependence that lies at the heart of all human needs for relationships, one becomes incapable of love, friendship, marriage, or any truly human co-operative activity.

I have suggested that some of the forms of character I commented on are 'infantile' or 'immature' in the relation they bear to modes of orientation and affective organization formed in childhood. Either the person has kept that orientation and organization, so that it governs or shows in the way he approaches and responds to contemporary situations; or his attitudes and responses represent his way of keeping at bay inclinations and unresolved conflicts embodied in these early orientations and organizations. In both cases emotional learning and development has come to a relative standstill. In the first case the person's immaturity finds expression in his actions, behaviour, affective responses and relationships; in the second case the form which all these take are at least partly designed to hide it.

'Infantile' means 'belonging to childhood' or 'like those found in childhood'. But this still raises the question about the way modes of response that we find in children differ from adult ones. Our difficulty is increased if we wish to say that many adult responses are themselves not very different from those of children (Guntrip, 1977):

> Even though the struggle to achieve freedom for independent
> action begins so early in childhood, the conditions of human
> existence make it an exceptionally difficult thing for the child to
> grow out of the infantile dependence of its earliest relationships
> to the mother and the father (p. 382). At the deepest mental levels
> this infantile dependence is not and cannot be completely out-
> grown. It persists as an unconscious factor even in the maturest
> adult. Every human being. . .struggles to maintain a transitory
> independence for a short space of time in the world of adult
> responsibility and satisfaction (p. 384).

What Guntrip suggests here is that how 'adult' a person really
is shows when he is emotionally involved, under stress or
threat, when he is in a crisis or is caught up with his defences
down. Under stress he may cling to the public aspects of his
everyday behaviour; or he may show a very different face —
he may become rash, inconsiderate, helpless. If he is genuinely
adult, he will be able to dispense with the public aspects of
his behaviour while retaining many of the qualities and values
that inform these — accountability, thoughtfulness, dependability, integrity. It is these qualities that are regarded as
'adult' because they can only be reached by a process of
emotional learning and development.

An 'immature' person is one who has not reached a state
of maturity, one whose development is held up. Of course
such a person will generally learn new things. For instance, he
may 'fall into bad company' and learn 'bad habits'. Here one
may ask: how does this differ from the case of a 'mature'
person learning from the people he looks up to? Does the
difference not lie simply in what they learn? I think that here
the nature of what they learn and the character of the learning
are inseparable. The difference between the two cases lies in
the fact that in the latter case the learning is a change in the
person — one can call it 'development'.[1] In the former case it
is a consolidation of the way he already is. Thus the bad ways

---

[1] It is, of course, also possible for what a person meets in life to destroy his
genuinely mature qualities. This too would be a change in the person, only in
the opposite direction. So we are left with the problem of describing what the
distinction between the two cases amounts to.

a person picks up from his friends become a vehicle for his early greediness, exercized in adult situations and with the kind of deliberation which would not have been possible without his adult accomplishments — intelligence, judgement, experience, and the taste for expensive goods and refined vices. In contrast, the mature person constantly discovers new difficulties in emulating what he admires or in performing well the tasks that absorb him. Each step forward, even if it brings him fulfilment, is a giving of a bit of himself. Learning here is neither a matter of taking over or appropriation, nor of copying or imitation, although at first there has to be copying, imitation and appropriation (i.e. 'identification' and 'introjection') before the young child can have a solid base from which to develop.

2 The Mature Person and his Character

I have suggested that we can divide forms of 'immature' character into three categories — reactive, narcissistic and impulsive — and that in the borderline region between the last two we have character traits we describe negatively, such as irresponsibility, recklessness, spinelessness. What we thus describe a person as lacking or as having failed to attain are aspects of emotional maturity. A person who has been unable to develop such aspects of character is one whose concern for other people is sporadic, one who is not constant in his relation to the values in which he believes, one who is subject to moods of depression and elation but whose capacity for experiencing deep joy or grief is limited, one who lacks critical judgement and is easily influenced. So, presumably, a mature person is one who has developed the qualities which such a person lacks.

Inevitably 'maturity' is a moral category and we have to use moral categories in elucidating what it means — such categories as responsibility, steadfastness, dependability, loyalty, seriousness, courage, integrity and others. I do not think, however, that the use to which psycho-analysis puts this notion makes the psycho-analyst morally partisan in the sense that the moral categories with which it is connected do not tie it down to any one specific set of values. The difficulties which a person's immaturity creates for him are not moral difficulties that are confined to any particular set of values. With suitable modifications one can imagine him believing in different values and still having the same difficulties. For they are difficulties bound up with limitations in his ability to give, to care, to stand fast, to remain consistent, to face danger, to exercise caution and prudence, to think for himself. If we are to describe any of these limitations as 'aspects of immaturity' then we must not forget that what gives each such an aspect is what else surrounds them in the character of the person who has them. This applies equally to 'aspects of maturity', unless we pick those aspects in terms of concepts that are already connected with the concept of maturity, such as responsibility and autonomy. But then we have the problem of elucidating what they mean.

So let me turn to one particular description of maturity — Reich's description of the 'genital' character which he regards as an ideal of maturity (Reich, 1950, p. 165): 'With regard to their qualitative differences the genital and the neurotic character are ideal types. The real characters are mixed types.' He means that his description is of an unadulterated form which does not exist in nature. This is connected with the claim to which I referred earlier that no men reach maturity or are completely mature: 'In actual fact human beings only approximate to it' (Guntrip, 1977, p. 363). Reich's description of the mature 'genital' character has many sides:

1 Such a person's infantile conflicts have been resolved. He has not remained stuck on, is not still over-attracted by infantile sexual pleasures. He does not look for or find his mother in the women who attract him; in the men he comes into contact with he does not see his father or look for qualities he was disappointed not to find in him. His dealings with people are not burdened with infantile conflicts.

2 He has a preponderance of good feelings — goodwill for others, concern, the capacity to trust (though not uncritically), honesty, the ability to give, forgive and appreciate. He is friendly, but not indiscriminate in his friendships. What he gives comes from him and counts for something. He is loyal

to his friends, steadfast in his affections, responsible in his actions and dependable. His good feelings make him outgoing and responsive to other people.

3   He is free from destructive and self-centred emotions. The psycho-analytic view is that these feelings — greed, envy and jealousy — are the lot of every child, and that love, concern for and interest in what is outside the self offers the possibility of outgrowing them. The inner security and fullness which develops through the give-and-take of love reduces envy, jealousy and the anxious readiness to take every frustration as an attack on the self. Here Melanie Klein speaks of the 'mitigation of hatred by love' (1957, p. 25). Thus the person who has outgrown his greed, envy and fear of persecution is neither spiteful nor vindictive. He does not enjoy cruelty and is not burdened by feelings of guilt. He can be angry without fear of doing irreparable harm. He is forgiving. He can accept the rewards of success without feeling he is outshining others. He can step aside without feeling he will be outshone. He can accept privation without feeling starved. He can respond to other people's demands without feeling exploited.

4   He is not concerned to defend himself, to guard against pain, to keep up appearances. He is free from duplicity and is direct in his dealings with people. He is not afraid to speak his mind, to be critical, to show his feelings. This is not incompatible with reserve. Certainly he does not flaunt his feelings and respects other people's privacy.

5   He is not afraid of his feelings and is capable of feeling things deeply. He does not protect himself by withdrawing into himself. Though not easily hurt or disappointed, his experience of pain, grief and disappointment is not muted. On the other hand he does not wallow in these feelings, feel sorry for himself. If he hurts or harms someone he feels sorry readily and is willing to make amends. The inner strength that comes with maturity thus allows for deeper contact with the environment, though it also leaves him vulnerable to pain. As Freud pointed out (1949b, pp. 319—20), 'there is *other* misery in the world besides neurotic misery — real unavoidable suffering', and freedom from neurotic conflict leaves a person exposed to real suffering. Dr Drury comments (1973, p. 22) that 'Freud showed real profundity when he stated that the

aim of psycho-analysis was to replace neurotic unhappiness by normal unhappiness'.

6   His inner security is not defensive or arrogant. He is secure in his identity and does not seek achievements as a compensation. As I said, he can bear privation without feeling deprived, pain without feeling persecuted, doubt without feeling lost, and loss without inner disintegration.

7   He has deep convictions, born out of love and regard for the people with whom he belongs, and the courage to stick to them when doing so is unpopular. But this courage 'is not a proof of potency' (Reich, 1950, p. 169). Whatever his convictions, he is not 'censorious' towards other people. I am thinking of a negative attitude, clad in moral clothes and born out of envy. His morality is free of sadism.

8   His interests are genuine, he is alive. He finds pleasure in life, though pleasure is never the end he seeks, it comes to him in the nature of a bonus. Thus, just as he is capable of deep sorrow, he is equally capable of intense joy. This too is part of the contact which his freedom from defensive measures and protective attitudes allows him to enjoy. Such contact is the antithesis of the 'insulation' which Reich's 'character armour' generates (Reich, 1950, p. 148).

9   He is self-disciplined, possesses self-mastery, although his self-control is the opposite of the kind of control which stifles spontaneity. Whether his actions are immediate or come from reflection, he is always behind them and his responses come from him. He thinks for himself and acts on his own behalf — though obviously this doesn't mean that he 'thinks of himself' or 'acts for his own sake'. He stands by what he says and does, and is ready to take responsibility for what flows from his actions — e.g. to justify them, to take the blame, etc.

This is the general picture or conception of emotional maturity which I have extracted from Reich. It is one which, despite other differences between different schools of thought in psycho-analysis, is embedded in psycho-analytical thinking. It is supposed to represent the form of existence and orientation towards which human beings strive to develop emotionally as individuals when not thwarted by the way in which their social environment impinges on this development.

We have seen that Freud regarded this influence as inevitably thwarting. He also overemphasized what in the young child makes for a reluctance to develop — 'the stickiness of the libido', its tendency to stick at pregenital positions. However differently psycho-analysts may understand the nature of this reluctance today, the fact remains that there is a reality which corresponds to it: development involves overcoming and outgrowing what anchors, freezes, fixes. Hence Freud's concept of 'fixation'. What constitutes a 'thwarting' impingement obviously varies with the stage of development, the age of the child, and his individual state of mind at that stage. Again there are different schools of thought in psychoanalysis with regard to the significance of the different stages regarding the future development of the individual. We have seen the significance which Freud attached to the Oedipus complex and its resolution. Reich keeps this emphasis in *Character Analysis*. Other psycho-analysts, notably Melanie Klein and Fairbairn, consider earlier stages and conflicts to be more important for the course of emotional development.

While retaining Freud's emphasis on the reluctance of the child to venture forth and develop, whether held back by something in which he finds pleasure (Freud, Reich), or by the security inherent in the early state of dependence (Fairbairn) and therefore, negatively, by the fear of independence, responsibility and freedom (Fromm), it is also important to take account of initiative and interests in the child and the way these enter into and contribute to his emotional development. Here it is the lack of 'impingement' of the social environment on his development that would 'thwart' that development through spiritual starvation. In any case, psychoanalysts emphasize the importance of maternal 'support', especially in the first year of life (Klein, Winnicott). Without such support the growing infant would be at the mercy of his own emotional reactions. Equally, if emotional development is to continue, it is important that this support should be gradually withdrawn at a later stage (Winnicott). Otherwise it would sap initiative and weaken the will for growth towards greater independence. Therefore to the dangers of deprivation in childhood one has to add those of over-protection, just as those of over-strict discipline have to be counterbalanced by the dangers of providing no discipline, nothing solid from which the child can take his bearings and in which he can find the expression of his parents' care for him.

I said that, whatever their differences, psycho-analysts broadly agree on the conception of emotional maturity I have sketched. This is true, for instance, of Erich Fromm, despite his sociological emphasis. He is obviously interested in the way a society's culture may 'thwart' the development of character in an individual while shaping his personality. Let me make it clear that while a society's culture inevitably shapes the personality of its members, it does not follow from this that it must 'thwart' their development. It is Fromm's contention, however, which I am not here concerned to discuss, that there are certain cultures where such thwarting is inevitable.[2] The conception of emotional maturity he develops in *Man for Himself* does not differ significantly from the one I have sketched. He calls it 'productiveness' and by this he means an orientation in which a person takes interest in what is outside himself, gives of himself to and works for it, in the knowledge of its needs. He does this freely, because he wants to, and what he does comes from him. He is thus not alienated from what he does. In so far as he lives his life in this way he is at one with himself. In his relationships he is not afraid to seek closeness and contact, but he keeps his own independence and respects the individuality of others.

Autonomy and initiative, authenticity, freedom from inner conflict and orientations of independence, outgoingness, interest in and contact with what is outside the self: these are the key concepts in terms of which Fromm develops his conception of 'the productive character'. Its affinity to Reich's conception of 'the genital character' is evident. Where he differs from Reich is in his rejection of Freud's account of emotional development in terms of the transformations of libidinal organization. It also has many points of contact with Fairbairn's conception of 'mature dependence' — 'characterised by equality, mutuality, spontaneity (lack of compulsion) and stability' (Guntrip, 1977, p. 359). The big difference lies

---

[2] He discusses this question in greater detail in Fromm, 1956.

in the levels at which each discusses the antithesis of this form of independence, namely 'infantile dependence' (Fairbairn) or 'symbiosis' and 'withdrawal' (Fromm), and their view of what constitutes the most important obstacles to be overcome in developmental progress towards maturity. Fairbairn, like Reich, attaches great importance to the young child's relations, going considerably further back than Reich, while Fromm focuses attention mainly on the individual's current interactions and their social setting.

3 Maturity and Morality

If we speak of 'the mature character' we have to recognize that we are not speaking of a particular kind of character. It is the person who is mature and this shows in his character. If the question is what kind of character is compatible with maturity, then the answer is that this admits of a great variety. For instance, a mature person can be meek, shy and reserved, or he can be bold and even aggressive. But arrogant? Why not?

It seems to me that a character trait which is burdened with infantile conflict is to that extent one that gives expression to the person's lack of maturity. But what is an infantile conflict? It is one in which infantile inclinations and attitudes are in conflict. And what makes an attitude infantile or childish? Its being a mode of response or relatedness which presupposes defenselessness, weakness, dependence, and a lack of recognition of or respect for the realities of the situation to which it is a response.

It is extremely difficult in reality to draw the distinction. An adult world, that is the world in which adults live, has plenty of adult problems, many of which it would be impossible for children to have or face — problems in political life, problems related to certain kinds of loyalty, moral problems which presuppose a certain kind of status and certain powers in the person who has it, marital problems, and so on. For instance, a man who is in politics and has risen to an influential position in the hierarchy of his party may be faced with problems to do with wielding power. He may have to fight to keep the power he has; he may have to persuade, coax and sometimes bully others. How he will behave will depend on what he wants to achieve, what this means to him, his judgement of a particular situation, his moral beliefs, and the kind of person he is — whether he is imaginative or limited in his vision, bold or cautious, etc. Within the variety possible here, we may be able to say of him that he is facing up to the adult problems in question in an adult way. We may be able to say that he is living in an adult world.

On the other hand we may have to qualify this statement. When and in what way may we wish to do so? For instance, if it turns out that he is in politics for the power he can acquire there, that he clutches it greedily and hangs on to it ruthlessly, that without it he would feel lost, I think that we may wish to revise our original statement. One who has and wields power will have the problem of keeping it. This may be a problem *in* politics, a problem *of* political life. When one who is involved in such a life faces this problem, the problem will be *his* and, therefore, personal in that sense. It is his belonging to that life which makes the problem his. His desire for power, the value which he places on it, come from that life. In our particular example we have imagined this desire to have more than one source. It comes partly from the politician's childhood; it may be the expression of an inability to reconcile himself to his own lack of power as a child of which, perhaps, he was made aware painfully by his elders. In so far as we can say that beneath the exterior of his current life he still feels as he felt then, as a child, small, and resentful at being made to feel so, we can say that his present problems carry the burden of his childhood conflicts, that there is more to them than meets the eye. If those conflicts had been resolved, he might still find power attractive and enjoy having it, but not in the same way.

The point is that he sees the problems of his current life in terms of categories that come from his childhood, categories which belong to emotions which he has not outgrown. Greed, for instance, involves a mode of consciousness in which other people are seen as instruments which provide the food one needs or as obstacles to that satisfaction. When other people satisfy one's needs they are seen as friendly and good. Where they continue to do so, the friendly and appreciative response in the way one relates to them is a form of love. But it is an immature form of love; it is the love of which an emotionally immature self is capable. For that love to change character the self has to outgrow its greed. Generally, as the child grows and learns from what he meets in life, he will outgrow the self-centred orientation that belongs to his greed. He will come to tolerate failures in his mother's attention, to appreciate that these failures do not have the devastating significance he attached to them. If, however, early deprivation is too severe, this will intensify his greed and anchor him in a self-centred orientation. When he grows up his recognition of other people's independent individualities will be tenuous. His greed will dominate his desire for whatever he needs. If, for instance, what he needs is power, then the way he hungers for, seeks and, once obtained, tries to keep it will bear the mark of his immaturity. He will rise to any situation that threatens to take it away from him with the self that belongs to the past and is orientated by its greed. I am suggesting that what it excludes can only be attained by 'emotional learning'. That is why I describe a person whose character is dominated by greed as immature. Socrates pointed out in the *Gorgias* that such a person lacks self-mastery.

A similar case can be made for arrogance, vanity, envy and avarice. They are all expressions of craving and can take the form of compulsion. Thus a person may be eaten up with envy, driven by the desire to spoil the things that are enjoyed by others. He may be driven by the desire to store and keep what he regards as valuable; he may be unable to part with any of it or share it with someone else. He may be driven by the desire to appear in the best light, to arouse other people's envy, to make other people feel small. In each case what is in question is what he wants, yet in his pursuit of it he acts in slavery to overpowering needs. That is why he cannot be said to have self-mastery. In contrast we cannot say that a person is driven by generosity. If he were, he would not be generous. There is such a thing as compulsive giving; but then the giving is a way of seeking something for oneself, whereas true generosity is an expression of love and concern.

Generosity is something one has to learn; meanness is not. If a child becomes meaner as he gets older then this is a snow-

balling of his reactions to a situation that continues to provoke anxiety. He is going downhill. On the other hand the
learning of generosity is what I called 'emotional learning'. I
am not suggesting that there are not unlearned, natural reactions of generosity in children. But these reactions have to be
co-ordinated and built on. They will only add up to generosity
with a growth of the self from which they come, a growth
involving the consolidation of a 'giving' orientation which
has thought for other people at its centre. It is a moving away
from impulsive action and involves the development of
responsibility and self-control. It is this that makes generosity
an expression of maturity.

What about cruelty and vindictiveness? We considered earlier
Freud's view of sadism or the propensity to enjoy inflicting
pain on others. A cruel person is one in whom this propensity
is pronounced, one who gives in to it. Compassion, on the
other hand, is not something to which one gives in. Again
most people, from childhood onward, exhibit natural reactions
of pity in the face of other people's suffering. But such reactions do not add up to compassion. It is true that a person
can give in to the pity he feels, but this is a form of passivity,
whereas compassion is an active form of engagement which
takes knowledge, direction and self-control. There is such a
thing as inflicting pain on someone 'out of necessity' and
without enjoying it. Ideally at least this is what punishment
ought to be.[3] There is also such a thing as genuinely considering some crimes to be 'unforgivable' without feeling any
personal animosity or vindictiveness towards those who
commit them. But while such moral attitudes are possible,
they are rare. They require a certain kind of moral purity in
the self which cannot be reached without self-knowledge.
Such an attitude is, of course, antithetical to Christianity
which believes in forgiveness. On the other hand, 'impersonal
cruelty' is a contradiction in terms.

I will admit openly that this reasoning tends to pull me
towards a conclusion which leaves a certain sense of uneasiness
in me, namely that evil always comes from a self that is

---

[3] I have discussed this elsewhere. See Dilman, 1976 and Dilman, 1979, chapter 5.

immature in one respect or another. Simone Weil has pointed out that there is a certain ease in doing evil, that even where the wrong-doer is active his activity necessarily takes the form of 'giving in' to the tendency towards evil in him: 'Those whom we call criminals are only tiles blown off a roof by the wind and falling at random' (Weil, 1968, pp. 176–7). In contrast, she says, one does not fall into good.[4] Though she does not explicitly refer to emotional maturity, she clearly thinks that where evil takes planning and even self-discipline and self-sacrifice, this is *qualitatively* different from the kind of self-discipline and self-denial that is at the heart of true goodness; for it is still a form of indulgence. She discusses the difference in terms of the distinction between acting from a 'high' motive and acting from a 'low' one — which is a moral distinction. My point is that the moral development of the self which makes it possible for a person to act from 'high' motives necessarily involves emotional growth and the development of autonomy.

Obviously goodness and maturity are not the same thing, although I find it difficult to imagine how a person can develop emotionally without coming to care for and believe in something outside himself he sees under the aspect of goodness. I have been led to the conclusion that he cannot be good if he has remained a child; for goodness cannot be copied. On the other hand, I believe that a genuine will to the good makes its appearance very early in childhood. This is something which is made plain in Melanie Klein's work, although Freud himself showed little appreciation of it. I said, 'he cannot be good if he has remained a child.' Certainly this is not to say that a child must be evil. From the claim that without maturity there cannot be true goodness it certainly does not follow that immaturity is a form of evil. But neither does it follow that a mature person must be good. A person can be mature, relatively speaking, and morally mediocre. He need not have what Simone Weil calls 'a love of the good' in him; not in any deep form. On the other hand, if he does evil, whether by imitation or inclination, this would come from an immature

---

[4] I have commented on this question elsewhere. See Dilman, 1979, chapter 9.

part of himself — from the need for approval, the craving for identity, envy, greed, cruelty, resentment, wounded pride, the desire for revenge.

Am I saying, then, that 'the truly mature person' is incapable of resentment, for instance? I have not said that there is such a thing as the fully mature person. This is a myth which is itself the product of childhood phantasies, on a par with 'the superman'. What I am saying is that if a person resents something that has been done to him and retaliates in kind, then he does descend to an immature level of action. For resentment is our response to an action which, in one way or another, makes us feel impotent. The main point I should like to make is that there is no person, however mature, who is immune from the propensity to such regression. In that sense, a mature person is certainly capable of being tempted into and actually doing evil. The inclination, however, comes from what is immature in him, even when it enters into action through the agent's regression.

Bibliography

Anderson, John, 1940. 'Freudianism and Society', *Austral J. of Psy and Philosophy.*

Cary, Joyce, 1961. *The Horse's Mouth.* Michael Joseph.

Dilman, İlham, 1973. 'Freud and Psychological Determinism', *The Human World.*

— 1974a. 'Paradoxes and Discoveries', *Wisdom: Twelve Essays* (ed. Renford Bambrough). Blackwell.

— 1974b. 'Philosophy and Psychiatry', *The Human World.*

— 1975. *Matter and Mind, Two Essays in Epistemology.* Macmillan.

— 1976. 'Socrates and Dostoyevsky on Punishment', *Philosophy and Literature.*

— 1978. 'Universals: Bambrough on Wittgenstein', *Arist. Soc. Suppl. Vol. 79.*

— 1979. *Morality and the Inner Life, A Study in Plato's Gorgias.* Macmillan.

— 1980. *Studies in Language and Reason.* Macmillan.

— Forthcoming *Freud's Conception of the Mind.*

Dostoyevsky, Fyodor, 1956. *Crime and Punishment* (trans. David Magarshack). Penguin Classics.

Drury, M. O'C. 1973. *The Danger of Words.* Routledge and Kegan Paul.

Fairbairn, Ronald, 1952. *Psycho-Analytic Studies of the Personality.* Tavistock Publications.

Frankl, Viktor E. 1967. *Man's Search for Meaning.* Washington Square Press.

Freud, Sigmund, 1933. *New Introductory Lectures on Psycho-Analysis* (trans. W. J. N. Sprott). W. W. Norton.

— 1948. *An Autobiographical Study* (trans. James Strachey). The Hogarth Press.

— 1949a. *Three Essays on the Theory of Sexuality* (trans. James Strachey). The Alcuin Press.

— 1949b. *Introductory Lectures on Psycho-Analysis* (trans. Joan Rivière). Allen and Unwin.

— 1949c. *Group Psychology and the Analysis of the Ego* (trans. James Strachey). The Hogarth Press.

— 1949d. *The Ego and the Id* (trans. James Strachey). The Hogarth Press.

— 1949e. *The Future of an Illusion* (trans. W. D. Robson-Scott). The Hogarth Press.

— 1949f. *Civilisation and its Discontents* (trans. James Strachey). The Hogarth Press.

— 1950. *Collected Papers* vols. i–v (trans. Joan Rivière). The Hogarth Press.

— 1954. *The Origins of Psycho-Analysis, Letters to Wilhelm Fliess, Drafts and Notes: 1887–1902* (ed. M. Bonaparte, Anna Freud, Ernst Kriss, trans. E. Mosbacker and James Strachey). Imago.

— 1965. *Totem and Taboo* (trans. James Strachey) Routledge and Kegan Paul.

Fromm, Erich, 1950. *Man for Himself*. Routledge and Kegan Paul.

— 1956. *The Sane Society*. Routledge and Kegan Paul.

Ginsberg, Morris, 1950. *Sociology*. Oxford University Press.

Guntrip, Harry, 1949. *Psychology for Ministers and Social Workers*. Independent Press.

— 1977. *Personality Structure and Human Interaction*. The Hogarth Press.

Horney, Karen, 1937. *The Neurotic Personality of Our Time*. W. W. Norton.

Jones, Ernest, 1937. 'Love and Morality', *The Internat. J. of Psycho-Analysis*. Jan.

— 1955. 'The Genesis of the Super-ego' (1947), *An Outline of Psycho-Analysis* (ed. Clara Thompson). A Modern Library Book.

— 1949. *What is Psycho-Analysis?* Allen and Unwin.

— 1974. 'Mother-Right and the Sexual Ignorance of Savages' (1924), *Psycho-Myth, Psycho-History*, vol. ii. Hillstone.

Jung, C. G., 1953. *Two Essays on Analytical Psychology* (trans. R. F. C. Hull). Routledge and Kegan Paul.

— 1966. *Modern Man in Search of a Soul* (trans. W. S. Dell and C. F. Baynes). Routledge and Kegan Paul.

Kant, Immanuel, 1959. *Fundamental Principles of the Metaphysic of Ethics* (trans. T. K. Abbott). Longmans.

Klein, Melanie, 1948. 'The Early Development of Conscience in the Child', *Psycho-Analysis To-day* (ed. Sándor Lorand). Allen and Unwin.

— 1952. 'Some Theoretical Conclusions Regarding the Emotional Life of the Infant', *Developments in Psycho-Analysis* (ed. Joan Rivière). The Hogarth Press.

— 1957. *Envy and Gratitude*. Tavistock Publications.

— 1960. 'Our Adult World and its Roots in Infancy'. Tavistock pamphlet.

Lawrence, D. H. 1934. 'St. Mawr', *The Tales of D. H. Lawrence*. Secker.

— 1977. *Fantasia of the Unconscious*. Penguin.

Leavis, F. R. 1967. 'Anna Karenina: Thought and Significance of a Great Creative Work', *Anna Karenina and Other Essays*. Chatto and Windus.

Mach, Ernst, 1898. 'On the Principle of Comparison in Physics', *Popular Scientific Lectures* (trans. Thomas J. McCormack). Chicago Open Court.

Macmurray, John, 1933. *Freedom in the Modern World*. Faber and Faber.

Malinowski, Bronislaw, 1955. *Sex and Repression in Savage Society*. Meridian Books.

Milner, Marion, 1977. *On Not Being Able to Paint*. Heinemann.

Money-Kyrle, R. E. 1955. 'Psycho-Analysis and Ethics', *New Directions in Psycho-Analysis* (ed. Melanie Klein, Paula Heimann, Roger Money-Kyrle). Tavistock Publications.

Nietzsche, Friedrich, 1972. *Twilight of the Idols* and *The Anti-Christ*. Penguin Classics.

Overstreet, Harry and Bonaro, 1954. *The Mind Alive*. W. W. Norton.

Plato, 1973. *Gorgias*. Penguin Classics.

— 1952. *Symposium*. Penguin Classics.

Proust, Marcel, 1952. *In Remembrance of Things Past* (trans. C. K. Scott Moncrieff). Chatto and Windus.

— 1954. *A la recherche du temps perdu*, vols. i—iii. N. R. F., Bibliothèque de la Plèiade.

Puner, Helen Walker, 1959. *Freud: His Life and His Mind*. Dell Publishing Co.

Reich, Wilhelm, 1950. *Character Analysis*. Vision Press.

Rhees, Rush, 1969. 'Religion and Language', *Without Answers*. Routledge and Kegan Paul.

— 1970. 'Wittgenstein's Builders' and 'Some Developments in Wittgenstein's View of Ethics', *Discussions of Wittgenstein*. Routledge and Kegan Paul.

— 1971. 'The Tree of Nebuchadnezzar', *The Human World*. August.

Robinson, Ian, 1975. 'Notes on the Language of Love I and II', *The Survival of English*. Cambridge University Press.

Sachs, Hanns, 1945. *Freud, Master and Friend*. Imago.

Segal, Hanna, 1964. *Introduction to the Work of Melanie Klein*. Heinemann.

Sophocles, 1968. 'King Oedipus', *The Theban Plays*. Penguin Classics.

Stocks, J. L. 1969. 'Desire and Affection', *Morality and Purpose* (ed. D. Z. Phillips). Routledge and Kegan Paul.

Suttie, Ian D. 1948. *The Origins of Love and Hate*. Kegan Paul, Trench, Trubner and Co.

Tolstoy, Leo, 1956. *Anna Karenina* (trans. Rosemary Edmonds). Penguin Classics.

— 1960. 'The Kreutzer Sonata', *The Kreutzer Sonata and Other Tales* (trans. Aylmer Maude). World Classics, Oxford University Press.

Weil, Simone, 1951. 'Lettre à une Elève' (1934), *La Condition Ouvrière*. Gallimard.

— 1953. *La Pesanteur et la Grâce*. Gallimard.

— 1959. *Waiting on God* (trans. Emma Craufurd). Fontana.

— 1968. 'Some Reflections on the Love of God', 'The Love of God and Affliction', *On Science, Necessity and the Love of God* (ed. and trans. Richard Rees). Oxford University Press.

Winnicott, D. W. 1957. *The Child and the Family*. Tavistock Publications.

— 1958. *Collected Papers: Through Paediatrics to Psycho-Analysis*. Tavistock Publications.

Wisdom, John, 1965. *Paradox and Discovery*. Blackwell.

Wittgenstein, Ludwig, 1963. *Philosophical Investigations*. Blackwell.

— 1967. *Zettel*. Blackwell.

Wollheim, Richard, 1971. *Freud*. Fontana.

Wortis, Joseph, 1954. *Fragments of an Analysis with Freud*. Simon and Schuster.

Index